BECOMING:
Journeying toward Authenticity

〜❧〜

Jill Schroder

Dedication

To my children, Lisl and Martin,
their children, Marlena and Lilly, Noah and Nick,
and to children and grandchildren everywhere;

to my parents, Gerrie and Joe,
grandmothers Jo, Maria, and Fran,
and to parents and grandparents everywhere;

to the mystery,
the source,
the ground of being from which all becoming arises.

Library and Archives Canada Cataloguing in Publication

Schroder, Jill, 1942-

Becoming: Journeying Toward Authenticity

ISBN 978-0-9812019-0-0

Published by **CONNECTING** ☯
Vancouver, BC, Canada
www.becomingthejourney.com

Cover and interior design: Trapdoor Media
www.trapdoormedia.com

Requests to reprint all or parts of Becoming should be addressed to
CONNECTING
1203-2055 Pendrell St.
Vancouver, B.C. V6G 1T9
Canada
Tel: 604 662-7561

CONNECTING is pleased to sponsor Families for Children.
A portion of proceeds will go to this organization.
www.familiesforchildren.ca

Table Of Contents

Acknowledgments

One of the many gifts that have come from compiling these essays has been a more conscious awareness of the people and places, the teachers and teachings, that have been significant components of my becoming. My gratitude abounds, and although the list can only be partial, I take pleasure in creating and sharing it.

In particular I remember and thank my mother, Gerrie, for her nurturing, love of children, attention to exercise, healthy food, and good posture; for owning her shadow sides and making it part of our family life to talk about everything—the interesting and pleasant, the dark and difficult topics alike; my father, Joe, for his unflagging support, loyalty to, and delight in me, for his help in countless projects, for his musical genius and inspiration, his unending interest in learning; my brother, Jim, for his and his wife Pat's generosity, for riding the ups and down together, for our banging of heads and hugging, for his commitment to good science and teaching; the grandmothers in my life, their laps, their loves, their wisdom, permission, and their cookies! Thanks to my husbands, first and present: Wolf for his passion for life, his loyalty and conviction that 'we were a team in spite of it all'; and to Mike for the innumerable ways he has contributed to my growth, capacity for acceptance, for pointing me toward meditation and spiritual work, and for the final, fine-tooth-comb proofreading of this manuscript; to my children, Lisl and Martin, for choosing me as their mom, and being traveling companions of the first ilk; and then also to all my grandchildren—whose gifts and contributions to my becoming are inestimable.

Thanks to Kathy Barnhart, John Davis, Gary Harper, and Wendy Hilliard, for their thoughtful and generous comments about this venture. Thanks too to Wendy, Adrianne Ross, Martine Charles, and Kathryn Templeton for reading parts or all of the manuscript and offering insightful suggestions; to Christina Baldwin, whose course and book on writing as a spiritual quest were an early stimulation for this work; to Carla Rieger, whose performance and writing were inspirational. Carla connected me with my editor, Gerda Wever-Rabehl, who then, fortuitously, became my publisher. Heartfelt thank yous to Gerda and The Write Room Press for offering a motivational blend of encouragement and challenge, inviting me to deepen my scope and expand my reach. And to Katie Bowden and Stephanie Murray of Trapdoor Media for their infinite patience, vision, and creativity, as we worked together on design and layout.

Many of the essays comprise wisdom and insights acquired, shared, or deepened during walks, hikes, and conversations with friends and colleagues. I thank Cary McDonald for decades of companionship, and treasure the pleasure and connection that has come from being each other's sounding boards; Lance Shaler for his eternal optimism, and enthusiastic embracing of alternative views that have enriched and challenged my own. To my women's group, the Web, our Dinner Group, and the Milieu Salon, gratitude and appreciation for the warmth and support as Becoming evolved.

During the almost two decades I was associated with the Justice Institute of BC, I was deeply enriched by the experiences of coaching and teaching collaborative conflict resolution. Thanks also to the many students whose enthusiasm, challenges, and feedback have contributed essentially to my becoming.

It afforded great pleasure to assemble the quotes that frame the individual essays. It also gives me joy to share with you, dear reader, the wealth of wisdom and experience that the related reading comprises. These works have been of the essence to me over the years. I warmly and deeply acknowledge those authors and scientists, philosophers, poets, thinkers and dreamers, psychologists, spiritual teachers and leaders, and others represented in this illustrious compilation for their contributions to my life and to Becoming.

To the students of the Diamond Approach, hailing from all corners of the globe, with whom the practice of inquiry and the sharing of retreats has enhanced and enriched my own unfoldment in untold ways, my respect, appreciation, and thanks.

Finally, a deep debt of gratitude extends to my spiritual teachers for the holding, support, the ongoing invitation to remain with my experience, to be curious about it, to ride and be the wave, to know and rest in the ocean of being. In particular, my appreciation and honour to A. H. Almaas, Hameed Ali, founder of the Diamond Approach, for his wisdom and compassion, for sharing his experiences of truth, of being, of true nature, that they may become accessible to others; to Tad Dick for his introduction to the Work, and to John Davis, Kristina Grondahl, Karen Johnson, Joyce Lyke, Carol Miller, David Silversteen—dear and precious teachers on this journey.

"*Writing isn't about making money, getting famous, getting dates, getting laid, or mak-ing friends. In the end, it's about enriching the lives of those who will read your work, and enriching your own life as well. It's about getting up, getting well, and getting over. Getting happy, okay? Getting happy. …Writing is magic, as much the water of life as any other creative art. The water is free. So drink. Drink and be filled up.*"
Stephen King

"*You are the storyteller of your own life and you can create your own legend or not…
Write what should not be forgotten.*" *Isabel Allende*

◦◦◦◦◦

Preface
Why me? Why Now? What about You?

About ten years ago I started making notes, some by hand, a few on my computer. I named the file 'Nuggets.' It contained thoughts, advice, wisdom from people in my life, some of whom I knew well, others who were teachers of us all. Aside from adding an occasional note or two, the file re-mained untouched for many years. I held the idea to flesh them out, but had not gotten further than to put together very brief snippets about merely a few of the nuggets. Until the summer of 2006.

We were in Berkeley in July of that year for the occasion of the gallery opening of my husband Mike's son, Nick Raynolds' one man show. We were staying with family, and Kathy, a good friend and person for whom I have deep respect, mentioned that she was enjoying writing her memoirs. Her comment stirred my curiosity and I asked how she happened to begin this form of writing. She said she'd come to realize that she wanted her children to know her from more than 'just' a child's perspective and as more than 'just' a mom. She'd taken a course in writing and she was greatly enjoying the writing.

She shared with me a personal chapter and said how much it had meant to her children, and what lovely conversations had grown out of it. I immediately flashed back to all the questions I wish I could have asked my own mother, questions to which I will never know the answers. I realized how much I would love to have read my mom's thoughts on what her life had been about, what she'd cared deeply for, learned, lost, regretted, celebrated, hidden, feared. I'd have been interested in what and whomever she might have chosen as themes.

So I began to entertain the notion of actually undertaking some personal writing. I did some reading on the topic, wrote out some suggested exercises. As I started to prepare notes about memorable events and experiences, I was thinking primarily of my own children as the audience. As the work developed, however, so did the context and potential readership. In their present form, the essays are intended as an invitation to children everywhere and to their parents. Mothers perhaps most directly, but fathers may also have wrangled with many of these issues, and are warmly welcomed as well. As is anyone who values reading, sharing, and reflecting on personal stories.

Becoming contains many teachings, tips and bits of wisdom, events, and experiences that have affected me deeply and helped shape the person I am now. Reflecting on, and sharing something of the flow of my life, I am still, and will always be, in the process of becoming, in search of what's real, my own authenticity.

The word 'becoming' has several other meanings that dovetail and complement the title, I find. Becoming can mean 'marked by suitability or appropriateness,' 'pleasing or attractive to the eye,' and can be 'used as a term for potentiality' in Aristotle's metaphysics. It also can imply 'moving on beyond states of being,' as expressed in the Dhammapada, an essential Buddhist scripture intended 'to instruct in the highest ends of life while simultaneously giving delight.' Past, present, future, philosophical and spiritual, all wrapped up into one.

Writing the essays for Becoming has been an active investigation into my values, history and assumptions, my very being. Writing these pieces became an adventure, an experiment, a challenge; it provided unexpected links and extended pleasure.

Several of the ideas and learnings came early in life, but many I would love to have been aware of much sooner. A hope in making these experiences explicit is that they may drop into your life at a felicitous time, that they may spark reflection, laughter, tears, and questions for you to ponder and pursue. They are an invitation for you to assemble and treasure your own nuggets and to share them as you see fit.

I believe, with Socrates, and without a doubt, that the unexamined life is not worth living. Sharing what has led to our individual growth and maturation, indeed to our becoming more authentic and whole, may perhaps contribute to that process, or a related one, in others. So I began, timidly at first. But before long I found myself getting swept along, finding enjoyment and wonder in recalling significant experiences and describing their meaning and relevance to me, and, as I see it, to our shared human condition. I find that the journey *is* the destination. May these tales kindle fires for you as well.

Related reading:

Baldwin, Christina (1991). *Life's Companion: Journal writing as a spiritual quest.* NY: Bantam Books
Dhammapada: The Path of Dhamma. (2005). *Anthology prepared by jtb for* Access to Insight: Free distribution http://www.accesstoinsight.org/tipitaka/kn/dhp/index.html
Dillard, Annie (1989). *The Writing Life.* NY: Harper & Row
McDonnell, Jane (1998). *Living to Tell the Tale: A guide to writing memoir.* NY: Penguin Books

"There is only one great adventure and that is inwards toward the self." Henry Miller

"I swear the earth shall surely be complete to him or her who shall be complete. The earth remains jagged or broken only to him or her who remains jagged or broken." Walt Whitman

Introduction
Filters and Frames

I had quite a trying and unsupportive childhood. My dad left for the army, basically abandoning me, when I was a few months old. My mother was insecure and anxious, rigidly bound to the parenting rules in vogue at the time. It seemed as if my parents didn't care what I wanted; they had rules to follow.

Actually, when I think about it, I've had a rather difficult life altogether. I was an only child for the first three years of my life, suffering loneliness often. Being alone terrified me for decades.

In high school I had a rotten time socially which colored the rest of my experience. I wasn't accepted into the social club I wanted, was never part of the 'in' crowd, had very few dates. I worked really hard; didn't play much in school, nor later in life either, for that matter.

When I finally fell in love it was with a foreigner, which created quandary after crisis with my parents. Our marriage was fraught with tension and disharmony. I won't go into the details, but let's just say my husband had a few habits that made my life painful and trying.

My parents died when I was only in my thirties. Hardly knew their grandkids. My mother-in-law was a controlling sort of virago, who always knew best. When someone else suggested something, her first response was nearly always a vehement 'no.' On top of all that, her food was overcooked and way too salty.

Becoming: Journeying toward Authenticity

As foreigners we were odd folks out in the small town in Europe where we lived. We never really fit in. We were Xs among the Os.

My marriage broke up and it was traumatic to leave so much behind and break up the family. I lay awake nights wondering if I had done the right thing, and had heart palpitations thinking of everything I was precipitating...

Here's another version:

My life has been blessed, maybe even charmed. I was a first child, so I had my parents' full attention for the important formative first years. Both parents adored me.

Actually, when I think about it, I have been extremely fortunate in numerous ways. I had a stable family life, especially in my adolescence when it matters so much. In high school I worked hard and loved it. I had a close group of girl friends. The five of us were inseparable, met for tea weekly, supported each other through all the bumps of adolescence. I won't recount here all the erotic adventures I've had, but they have added spice and left many fond memories!

As US citizens living in Europe during my first marriage, our family was always a little bit different. My son in particular relished being an X among Os.

Life with my first husband was a roller coaster with many positive dimensions. When our marriage came to an end we parted company quite amicably, have remained good friends to this day and enjoy vacationing together with our grown children.

My parents' deaths were untimely and hard, but the financial flexibility that I had as a result opened doors for the children and me. I am extremely grateful for this. And my mother-in-law has been a model for me in many ways. Her food was flavorful, real down home cookin'. The kids loved it.

When I started a new life in my mid forties, I found a satisfying niche for myself and finally felt like I was beginning to grow up.

Get the gist?

When we search in our psyches for our history and our stories—to recount to others, children or grandchildren perhaps, or to make sense of the past and present of our lives—we come across many pageants and scenes, numerous chapters and plays. And we can tell them in many ways.

Each of the above stories is *true* in its own way. Each one captures something actual and accurately reflects a part of my experience. The feelings, sounds, colors, people, actions are all there, stored in my memory. This is true for both the 'down' and the 'up' versions.

Yet reading the two versions we are left feeling as though we had just read about two completely different lives. What's the difference in the two sets of stories? The teller's filters and frames in the two versions are diametrically opposed. We can ask ourselves: Where does the teller put her attention? What does she notice and emphasize? What does she bring forward and into focus for her and the world to see? Does the person perceive the cup of life to be generously full or rather piteously empty?

We are continually choosing filters and frames for our lives, whether we know and acknowledge it or not. And we have the option, if we are conscious, to choose filters that contribute to our growth and maturation. We can become masters of how we frame our experiences, selecting filters that serve us, frames which fittingly reflect what we would like to emphasize, see and address.

Don't make the mistake of underestimating or minimizing the power of these choices: they resonate throughout our whole being. A choice is something active, even if we make it unconsciously. It works in and on us. The choice of the way we frame our life, on any given day, around any given issue, affects our mood, the way we hold our past, how we see the present, how we are likely to respond in the future.

Yet regardless of how one might answer these questions— whether we tend to emphasize the 'half-full' experiences or rather to focus on the 'half-empty' version—there is another, deeper, truth. No set of stories is the whole picture. My life is, our lives are, not this story *or* that story. They are this one *and* that one. Our realities, our stories, our lives are a blend of all the stories we could ever tell, weaving together, creating a fabric. There's no end, as long as we live, and who knows about what happens after that?   Perhaps our lives are a never-ending story, open-ended, part of a larger flow emanating from something mysterious, not separate from it, yet distinct and particular, unfolding in our unique location and manifestation. No one really knows.

What we can say with confidence is this: While we live, our stories themselves provide a vehicle that can help us appreciate and learn from our part in the flow. Telling them can shed light on times, places and events that perhaps existed only vaguely, shrouded in the mists of our memories. They can provide insights, epiphanies, evoke laughter and tears. They can give meaning and allow us to put our lives into radically new and unexpected perspectives. We can do this in our own heads, or in a journal, and take considerable benefit. Yet having a witness, someone to be with us as we explore and recount our experience of our lives, has the potential to deepen both the telling, and the effect of the tale, exceedingly.

As valuable as it is to use stories to share and understand our lives, I believe there's a certain risk in the telling of our stories, (as well as a certain risk in *not* telling them). There is the possibility that we can 'get stuck' in them. We can literally 'take ourselves to be' our stories: the one who was abandoned, or the one who started a new life in middle age, the odd one out, or... When we define ourselves by our stories, when we identify ourselves as the characters who had these and those experiences, to whom this and that happened, we run the risk of imbuing our lives with a kind of static, unchanging quality. We are basically living in the past.

'But isn't it *true* that we *are* our stories?' you might demur. In part, yes. We have become who we are now in part because of what we have experienced in the past and these experiences comprise our stories.

Yet I believe we can begin to free ourselves, gradually, to be sure, but steadily, from our stories. We can move toward being genuinely authentic and simply present, open to what is arising in the moment in a new, fresh way. Spiritual traditions talk about this: 'The present moment is all we have,' they say, 'all there is.' These wisdom traditions point to the possibility of being present, living in the now, no longer encumbered by the albatrosses of the limitations, pain, and burdensome beliefs about our past, and free from doubts and worries about the uncertainty of the future.

It is a rare human being who will become what some spiritual traditions call self-realized or enlightened, living then as pure presence, in and as our true nature. This is elusive, and most of us will not come close, at least in an ongoing way in our daily lives. Nor can we get there by wanting or trying. Yet with grace, a delicate balance of attention and affection, we might perceive a glimpse or sense of this quality without being able to hang on to it. Yet even one glimpse can be a splash of light that may guide and direct us.

Clearly we all have our stories, and it can be liberating and informative to tell them, to reflect on them, to share them. So how can we tell our stories and live in the present? How can we have the delight and relief, the pleasure, the healing that come with the recounting of our histories and not be bound or determined by them?

We can in some way, not entirely explicable, absorb our stories and experiences. They can become part of us, be inside us, without limiting or bounding us. It seems to me that this can happen when, in addition to 'telling' our stories, we can 'digest' them, begin to detach from them, learn from them. When we do not cling to them, they can help us become richer, deeper, wiser. By reflecting on who we were then, we begin a process of discovering who we have become through our life experiences. We can move toward presence and authenticity in part by becoming cognizant of our stories, the filters and frames we use to tell them, by learning from them and beginning to detach from them. We are basically 'metabolizing' the stories, the experiences. We can let go of the accounts per se, because we have been able to extract the nutrients, and we can let them nourish us today, now, here, in present time on our own personal journey.

Related reading:

Almaas, A. H. (1988). *The Pearl Beyond Price: Integration of personality into Being: An object relations approach.* Berkeley: Diamond Books

Baldwin, Christina (1991). *Life's Companion: Journal writing as a spiritual quest.* NY: Bantam Books

Davis, John (1999). *The Diamond Approach: An introduction to the teachings of A. H. Almaas.* Boston: Shambhala

King, Stephen (2000). *On Writing: A memoir of the craft.* NY: Simon & Schuster

Remen, Rachel Naomi (2006). *Kitchen Table Wisdom: Stories that heal.* NY: Penguin Books

*"The hardest years in life are those between ten
and seventy." Helen Hayes (at 73+)*

"Don't go back to sleep." Rumi

Growing Up

Related reading:
Almaas, A. H. (1986). *Essence: The Diamond Approach to inner
realization.* York Beach, ME: Samuel Weiser, Inc.
Dillard, Annie (1987). *An American Childhood.* NY: Harper & Row
Fulghum, Robert (2003). *All I Really Need to Know I Learned in
Kindergarten.* NY: Random House
Sandburg, Carl ((1922). *Rootabaga Stories.* NY: Harcourt Brace & Co.

*"We can easily forgive a child who is afraid of
the dark; the real tragedy is when men are afraid
of the light."* Plato

*"You have to do your own growing no matter how tall your
grandfather was."* Abraham Lincoln

∾ᘓᘐᗛ

Cutting the Mustard

It is a characteristically human habit to cling to a story, a view, an experience. A corollary of this habit of mind is that it becomes a fixed frame through which we perceive the world. Unquestioned, our stories become unconscious boxes: they trap us, hold us, bind us, and we don't even know it.

Here is an example. I was about three years old. My parents had company for dinner. On this special occasion I was allowed to come down to the dining room where the guests were sitting at the table. There was pleasant chatter.

I spied something on the table that caught my eye. It was in a shiny bowl. I reached up to touch it, put my finger in the container. Licked it. It was bitter and unpleasant. It burned my tongue, and made my face scrunch up in disgust and distaste. Everyone laughed, and I was deeply affected. Hurt. Humiliated. Confused. I didn't know any of those words, but I knew the feelings, in my body, my psyche, my gut. I felt like sinking into the floor and disappearing, to escape from the embarrassment and confusion. But I couldn't. I stood as rooted to the floor and they were laughing. Never mind that it was probably just a brief flutter of light, harmless humor, no matter that they probably found me adorable. My experience was that they were laughing *at* me and it was one of the most significant negative emotional experiences of my early life.

That particular experience of tasting mustard became a filter through which I interpreted many difficult life experiences. I marvel at how a single, brief event in a child's life can carry such psychological weight. In my first counseling session the mustard story featured prominently. Years later doing body work, it was the mustard story I told first. The impression and fear of being humiliated lasted and lasted. For much of my life, during challenging times, it was common that I returned to being three years old. The filter of feeling ostracized and humiliated was always lurking nearby, waiting to descend, to tint and taint the picture.

The way the mustard experience lodged in my psyche went something like this: I was beside the table, small and below the guests, and seemingly abandoned by my parents, (for I have no recollection of my parents at all). Either they were laughing at me too, because I was small and cute, or maybe mom was in the kitchen preparing hollandaise sauce, and dad in the living room tending the fire. I don't know. In any case neither they, nor anyone else came to my rescue. From my perspective, the moment lasted an eternity. I was alone, isolated, helpless, hapless, and, an important factor in my memory is that I felt humiliated. Of course I didn't verbalize this, or have any clear, differentiated sense of this at three. But it became my story.

It took me years of reflection and personal work to see that my interpretation of that experience was just that, an interpretation. It may be true that laughter at the dismay of a small child is not appropriate. I believe this is true, and have this in mind when my grandchildren do something 'cute' that causes them distress.

At the same time, what interests me today is that a single, brief, experience could carry such psychological weight and hold me in its grasp so strongly and for so long. The realization was more penetrating when I perceived that in this interpretation I was seeing myself as a victim. 'They' were doing something hurtful to 'me.' I had no power, no responsibility, no autonomy in the situation. In my interpretation, I was completely at effect. Again, this was all true for the three year old. She was at the effect of the adults then. But I carried this view of life, and my hard times, well into my forties. The mustard incident was indeed a 'significant emotional experience' (SEE) on the 'timeline' of my life.

When, after almost 50 years, I expanded my perspective, not so much to see that particular experience differently (because I was indeed small, innocent and had been laughed at), but to realize that I was not inherently, inalterably a victim, a major shift occurred. I did not need to feel humiliated when others disagreed with me, when I had done something that did not please, or even when I looked or felt awkward.

It took many years to let go of the story, not so much to tell it differently, but for it to lose its power over me. The time finally came where the SEE was no longer writ in capital letters, did not form the frame for the pictures and events in my life.

When we are able to break loose, to free ourselves from the psychic grip we have on our stories, and they on us, we can look more objectively at the ways we tend to hem ourselves in. When we start to drop or 'digest' what we have habitually told ourselves and others, the transformations that can happen are nothing short of miraculous.

Now that it does not hold me in its clutches any more, I smile at the mustard story. And try assiduously not to laugh *at* young people.

Related reading:
Faber, Adele and Elaine Mazlish (1999). *How to Talk So Kids Will Listen & Listen So Kids Will Talk.* NY: Collins
James, Ted and Wyatt Woodsmall (1988). *Time Line Therapy and the Basis of Personality.* Cupertino, CA: Meta Publications
Mahler, Margaret (1975). *The Psychological Birth of the Human Infant: Symbiosis and individuation.* NY: Basic Books
Murdock, Maureen (1990). *The Heroine's Journey: Woman's quest for wholeness.* Boston: Shambhala
Nelson, Jane (1981). *Positive Discipline.* Fair Oaks, CA: Sunrise Press

Reflections: What childhood event would you call a 'significant emotional experience' on your life's timeline? Has it been, or is it still, limiting for you? If so, in what ways? Take some time to experiment with telling the story in a different way. What do you notice in your body? How do you feel when you consider 'dropping' the old version of the story and adopting a new one?

"Each individual woman's body demands to be accepted on its own terms." Gloria Steinem

"Why hope to live a long life if we're only going to fill it with self-absorption, body maintenance, and image repair? When we die, do we want people to exclaim, "She looked ten years younger," or do we want them to say, "She lived a great life!" Unknown

A Weighty Matter

Our bodies do not enjoy the privilege and safety of personal privacy. They are often, and frequently painfully, in the public domain and subjected to the cruel and unflinching scrutiny of the public eye. The media, fashion models and advertising images create cultural norms under the burden of which many women feel trapped and enslaved. What is the effect of this tyranny? What can be done about it? As I reflect on these questions for myself and many women I know, I am transported to my early years.

My body was subject to the scrutiny of my mother, who was slim and had an abhorrence of extra pounds, as did her mother before her and the dominant culture in which they both lived. I think I was about ten years old when I learned that the way I looked was not acceptable. The message was none too subtle. I 'got it' that I was seen as too round, too heavy, too fat. I was even taken in for some tests. I remember sitting in the hall of the doctor's office, feeling isolated, and worried about what might to happen.Once the doctor called me in with the results of the tests, I sat anxiously on the edge of the chair, my mother beside me, listening intently. I was to be put on a diet, and even milk, which I loved, was to be excluded. My face burned, and I burst into tears. I felt ashamed but also indignant. I didn't measure up, and now was being punished. At a deeper level, which I did not yet fully understand, I knew that I was not meeting my mother's expectations. The fact that my thyroid values were on the low end of normal came as good news for my mother. There was a reason for my unacceptable roundness, and perhaps it could be fixed by taking a pill.

Looking back I know that I was not seriously overweight then. And never have been. Yet for the next 40 years, my weight took up an excruciatingly large space in my awareness.

For a long time, I believed that happiness could be found on the scale as I weighed myself each morning. If the scale were below a certain point, my heart lifted. I was convinced if I could only get my weight down far enough, people would like me, and life would finally really start. Things would be better. This focus on obtaining a certain weight meant that I was often focused on the future, pinning my hopes on a time when I would have lost the several pounds. I was dreaming of the day I would feel good about my body, when I would be slim and happy. Improved. Complete.

I remember sitting on the steps one warm summer day. I was a teenager. Starting on a diet again. I counted the green grapes that I could have. Wrote out the calories that the cottage cheese and carrots would add. I wanted be able to do something now to make things happen, to actively take charge of becoming thinner. I longed to make it happen fast, to have my actions show measurable results soon. But I realized that there was nothing I could do but not eat. And this not eating had to last for a long time—weeks, months. Amidst my renewed resolve to stick to the diet this time, I felt a sinking feeling, a kind of powerlessness. I felt like I ought to be able to control myself, my body. I did not yet know that an ebb and flow of pounds was normal and natural. I was grappling with a limited and distorted notion of what was attractive and acceptable that still lies deeply embedded in our western culture.

Decades later, when I inadvertently came across a letter I had written home from a summer camp, I saw the dramatic way I had internalized my mother's values. I winced as I read how I berated myself, said how weak I was, how bad I felt. I even apologized to my parents that I was unable to keep from eating the cinnamon rolls at Sunday breakfast, and that I had had a second blueberry pancake on Saturday. I told them how much I wanted to be good, and how hard I was trying. And I promised that when I got home, I would be better and start again. And maybe by the time school started, I could lose the pounds I had gained at camp through my weakness and failure of will.

It takes colossal courage to break familiar family patterns regarding what's spoken about, who calls shots, whose word counts. I didn't have that kind of courage then, nor for a long time. It is sometimes a whole life's journey to find our own values, not to take on the expectations of our parents, and to dare to stand up for ourselves and make our own way. It can be almost scary to make our own choices about how we want to look, feel, be when they contradict, or do not align comfortably with those around us. I grew up in the age of Twiggy, a high fashion model at the time, and very likely anorexic. What a challenge to make one's own body weight choices under the onslaught of 'thin images' which were widespread then, and still are today.

Not until well into middle age did I begin to acquire a more balanced view. I began to notice when I was being critical (even if I didn't say anything) of others' weight, saw how I was projecting my values and self-criticism. That has slowly begun to shift. Another shift has been to start each day with gratitude and an acceptance of what is, instead of being a slave to the scale. I thank my husband and his fundamental acceptance of my body as it is, for encouraging this shift. And I thank my mother for instilling healthy eating habits, and love of exercise, if not healthy attitudes regarding weight and body image. I feel good, look fine. I know now that happiness does not depend on plus or minus a few pounds on the scale, as I believed and lived for decades.

My appreciation and thanks to all the women who have written about the manifold negative effects that advertising, programming, and skinny cultural norms have had on female self-esteem, health, and well-being. And a reality check: obesity is a serious health hazard, and needs to be addressed. In my case, however, my weight was a significant emotional obstacle because I accepted and internalized others' standards, and it remained so until I was finally able to free myself from this burden. More or less.

Standards and expectations can come in many forms. A heavy one for me was weight and body image.

Related reading:

Brown, Byron (1998). *Soul Without Shame: A guide to liberating yourself from the judge within.* Boston: Shambhala
Gilligen, Carol (1993). *In a Different Voice: Psychological theory and women's development.* Cambridge: Harvard University Press
Kater, Kathy (2004). *Real Kids Come in All Sizes: Ten essential lessons to build your child's self-esteem.* NY: Broadway Books
Williamson, Marianne (1993). *A Woman's Worth.* NY: Ballantine Books

Reflections: What have been your challenges, if any, with standards imposed by family, friends or culture? Consider several standards imposed on you regarding body image, weight, self-esteem. Where did the values originate: at home, in the media, from cultural norms? How have you dealt with the issues as you have matured? What, if anything, might you like to address at this point in your life?

Becoming: Journeying toward Authenticity

"There is no end to the opening up that is possible for a human being." Charlotte Joko Beck

"You can outdistance that which is running after you, but not what is running inside you." Rwandan proverb

Expectations

'You must live up to your potential' was a phrase I heard early and often. It was a directive engraved in capital letters on my young soul. This is perhaps understandable given the household in which I grew up, mid–century, middle class, middle America. Also a natural extension of the performance driven way of life so widely accepted in that day and place. There was a certain noblesse oblige in it as well. After all I had been given many gifts: reasonable intelligence, health, above average resources and opportunities. So it made sense that I had a lot of potential to live up to. And that was that. For a long time.

For years I never questioned the philosophy or the values implicit in the phrase. I didn't think much about it, but I accepted it nevertheless. As I began to reflect on life purpose and my unique possibilities it came more clearly into focus how a certain expectation had been with me for ages. But I didn't know what my potential was, or what living up to it might mean, look, or feel like. There was a murky sense that potential is something you have and you're supposed to use it. I also believed that I was supposed to produce something to show for the effort. 'Living up' was a vague, yet ponderous 'should' hanging over my head, feeling at times like a crushing weight.

Mid-way through my post secondary education, I went to Europe on an exchange program where I met a number of students in circumstances similar to mine, about to complete their education and launch into their lives as young adults. I was a math major at a liberal arts college, but had no idea of what I might do with my life, not even what job I might like.

The students I met on the exchange program conveyed a certainty and dedication for the work for which they were preparing that was wholly unfamiliar to me. In contrast, I felt uncertain and inadequate. I didn't like my major much. I wasn't very good at it either, but felt stuck in it. Even more distressing was that I didn't know what I'd like to do instead. I could have switched majors, but there was no other area to which I was drawn. This stood out in painful contrast to the young Europeans, who seemed so well educated and unambiguous as they headed toward specific careers. They knew what they were about, where they were going.

After my math degree, I took the equivalent of an English major. But the graduate assistantship I accepted soon after made it clear to me that I was not interested in academic English as a niche, career, or even as temporary employment. As a young mother in Europe, and not having a direction of my own, I thought I might try what I saw other Europeans friends doing—interpreting folk tales, or interior decorating in the local, rustic style. But I found no fit.

I took courses in computer programming and statistics to help my student husband finish his degree. I could see that I had some talent here, but it was not my passion, not rewarding, like 'living up to my potential' surely would be. The inner critic continued its regular murmuring in my ear in its surly, frosty voice. It insinuated that whatever I was doing was not good enough. Not good enough for me, and certainly not when measured against what others were doing.

When I received my alumnae magazine in the mail after

graduating from college, I always flipped first to read the Class Notes. I looked forward with curiosity and interest to see what my classmates were up to. But inadequacy and hopelessness regularly oozed into me when I saw that women 'just like me' were president of this, leader of that, had been nominated for this award, invented that, were making waves and contributions. The 'normalcy' of my life haunted me. I was nothing special, had done nothing that stood out. No indication anywhere that I was living up to anything at all, let alone my full potential.

At such times, the voice would pop up from the subterranean recesses where it hid out on normal days and I would feel incomplete and inadequate all over again. The words and the voice led me to measure myself critically against others, but it also kept admonishing me to measure myself against all those gifts I'd been given and resources I had at my disposal. 'Not cutting it, Jill,' the voice would keep saying.

In the middle of my struggles there was a light spot. It didn't help *me* much, but was the beginning of a shift in perspective. My daughter, Lisl, had just turned 13, when I realized the damage that the comprehensive set of expectations laid on me by my familial, educational, and cultural circumstances had done to my capacity for contentment. As that realization sunk in, I made a commitment to myself and my daughter. I would lay off laying expectations on her. At least as much as I was able at the time.

As a parent I struggled to find the magic mixture of unconditional love, and firm, appropriate, guidance through rough channels; the blend of unqualified acceptance and assertive encouragement. The quest was the subject of much midnight anxiety, and continues to be the topic of many books on parenting. While I didn't, and wouldn't ever, have a complete and final answer, at least I had a good counter-example, and knew what I *didn't want* for my daughter—to be subject to the weight of familial expectations as I had been.

As the decades passed I began to question more intently

the validity of the slave driver that had pushed me relentlessly, allowing little peace or respite. I began to recognize the fallacy of seeing 'potential' as something concrete, specific, that could be 'lived up to.' It was an artificial construct, a formulation that was jarringly limited and harshly limiting. This questioning was accompanied by a breath of freedom from the inexorable voice. The insight even made me smile. More important, it created a gap between me and the voice. Gave me some space.

I started to detach, if ever so slightly from the lens and expectations of my parents, who, themselves, had never felt that they had lived their lives well. It was a poignant letting go, and I began to accept that I might just be a normal, average human being, whatever that means and however miraculous that is.

While the battle was far from over, there came a time when a different inner voice started to emerge, talking back to the inexorable one. This new voice had a slightly whiny, defensive timbre, but it was part of a gradual shift. I started questioning which accomplishments 'count' and why. I started to wonder about the meaning of success. But it was not until well into my sixties that I began to come upon a deeper resolution that had eluded me for decades.

It was as though an elegant key were now opening a deeper door to a locked and secret place. The key was the spiritual dimension. I came to understand what it means to 'live up to one's potential' in a more profound and meaningful way. Every human being inhabits a body, lives in a particular time and place. One could say we are of the earth, in this reality. *Yet* within each of us is the possibility of complete realization, enlightenment, expanding far beyond our usual, ordinary confines. In principle, if not in practice, we are unlimited. When I first glimpsed this new perspective, it was like tasting an exotic elixir. As human beings, we have the possibility of being *in* the world but not *of* it. We have the possibility, the potential of living our lives as a journey toward authenticity, as human beings and beings of spirit.

There is no more complete way, I have come to believe, neither as a baker, politician, candlestick maker, musician, patron, achiever of this, prize winner of that, that we can be more truly be living up to our potential, than by journeying toward authenticity.

Related reading:

Almaas, A. H. (2008). The *Unfolding Now: Realizing your true nature through the practice of presence.* Boston: Shambhala

Drew, Naomi (2000). *Peaceful Parents, Peaceful Kids: Practical ways to create a calm and happy home.* NY: Kensington Books

Kornfield, Jack (1994). *Buddha's Little Instruction Book.* NY: Bantam Books

Mauer, Robert (2004). *One Small Step Can Change Your Life.* NY: Workman Publishing

Nisargadatta, Sri Maharaj (1973). *I Am That.* Durham, NC: Acorn Press

Reflections: *List one expectation that you learned from your early environment that still guides you today. Where do you experience its effect on you in you attitudes, in your body? Does it serve you well or ill? What is an expectation that you did not 'live up to'? How do you feel about this? What relationship do you have to expectations in general at this time in your life?*

*"Manners are a sensitive awareness of the feelings
of others. If you have that awareness, you have
good manners, no matter what fork you use."* Emily Post

*"Nobody can make you feel inferior
without your permission."* Eleanor Roosevelt

~ ∾ ↄ

Tea with the Queen

One winter afternoon when I was about nine, after we had baked cookies together and a fire was crackling, my mother called me over to her. She seemed intent, and I felt a bit anxious. My brother, Jamie, and I looked up at her with curiosity and I felt my spine tingle. She said "Jill and Jamie, I want you to know that you are just as good as anyone else. There is no one you will ever meet where you need feel uncomfortable. You can hold your heads up and simply be yourselves in anyone's company." I was puzzled and didn't really know what to make of the speech and looked away, relieved that it wasn't something I'd done wrong. But she carried on: "You don't need to feel awkward or inferior meeting a president, a prize athlete or any other person of fame or fortune. You can feel perfectly comfortable having tea with the Queen."

I didn't make much of the message then, and turned to see if I could have another cookie. But the words seeped into some cranny of my memory, and they have re-emerged at intervals along my personal journey toward authenticity, as pointers to the possibility of self-acceptance and a sense of basic adequacy, even in difficult times.

My mother had grown up in very comfortable circumstances, physically as well as financially. She lived in large houses designed

Becoming: Journeying toward Authenticity

and built by her father, she had servants, went to private schools, and her family had fancy automobiles before most ordinary folks had a model T.

Gerrie's emotional landscape, in contrast, was rather bleak. While she never talked much about the challenging details of her youth, I discovered that her childhood scrapbook consisted mostly of letters or drawings she created for her parents while they were away for the evening, having gone off to the city (New York) for the theater, or to a concert.

We looked at the scrapbook together one day. "I remember my mom and dad going out for the evening," she said. "They were all dressed up, waved goodbye and were gone. I was left alone. Again." That was all she said. I filled in the picture as I looked at drawing after drawing with childish stick figures and awkward writing saying 'Welcome home. I missed you. I hope you had a good time. I love you and wish you were here...' and numerous variations on that theme.

I'm touched even today by the poignant contrast between my mom's comfortable beginnings, her message of confidence to Jamie and me, and the lonely drawings in the scrapbook and her own lack of confidence and sense of value. She once told me she dreamed that she had just arrived at a party. "I am always nervous about meeting people," she said, "but it was worse in the dream than I usually imagine. Everyone, even my friends, completely ignored me. I tried to say hello, but people just turned away. It was devastating, Jill. My heart was pounding when I awoke. It was a nightmare."

Given her challenges in these areas, I, in retrospect, admire her encouragement for us to be ourselves, to hold our heads up, feel comfortable at any time, at any place.

I recall a particular event where mom's message was in dramatic contrast to my experience, and where the words began to come alive and loom as a question rather than a statement. I was living in Europe at the time, mother of two small children.

I received an invitation to attend a reception in Switzerland that my Alma Mater was hosting, to be held in an alumna's home. As soon as I decided to go, I began to worry inordinately about what to wear. I struggled, for example, over which color combinations and accessories would go well. I fussed exceedingly on details of fashion that were otherwise completely unimportant to me. My world in Europe was long on family activities, spending time outdoors, and short on formal social situations.

I heard mom's words, echoing inside my head, reassuring me that I could feel comfortable with people in any circumstance. But I didn't get it. How could I feel relaxed when I felt incomplete and ill at ease? Self acceptance? Intrinsic adequacy? Such states were far away from how I felt anticipating the reception: awkward, bumbling, out of place. These were familiar feelings from my childhood, and ones that had accompanied me most of my life so far. During the train trip to Switzerland I continued to worry. Feeling the knots in my stomach, my sweaty palms, I began to be curious about the worry. Where did it come from? Why did I care so much?

As I pondered these questions on the train, I began to perceive mom's message at a deeper level. Her words had, in some way, been primarily about entitlement, about the external aspects of privilege and class: good education, upbringing, resources... these stood me in good stead for any situation, she'd meant. What I was grappling with now, and cared more deeply about, was my own personal sense of adequacy, or lack thereof: my fears of not being enough, not knowing enough, not being accepted or acceptable.

What does it actually mean to be comfortable 'being myself' and is simply being myself 'good enough'?

At that point I still cared desperately what people thought about me, how they perceived me. So many of the world's messages enforce this view: 'It's how you look, what you have that matters.' 'It's not who you are, but who you know that's important.' 'Buy this, accumulate that, get connected here, be seen there and you'll be richer, better, happier...'

I'm finally learning that in the complex blend of inside and outside circumstances which make up our lives, it's the inside knowing and valuing that lie deeper and closer to the truth of what real value means, and what would indeed let me have tea comfortably with anyone at all.

'Being myself' to me means coming to accept myself in a whole range of life situations and in the face of all exterior 'inadequacies' or shortcomings. It includes accepting my limitations, my inadequacies, my awkwardnesses, what I'm feeling, whether it be love or hate, fear or peace. It also includes allowing myself to really experience this range of feelings and ways of being.

My son is a pilot, and he tells me that an airplane flying from point A to point B is rarely precisely on course. My life, like a flight, is an ongoing series of course corrections, responding in the moment to feedback or my own awareness that I've veered off track. Learning to take others' views or judgments of me with a grain of salt, even when I may have gone 'off track,' to depend less on outside validation for my sense of self worth—these also comprise what it means to be myself.

Accepting and being myself doesn't mean that I won't make mistakes, have things to learn, or be unprepared at times. I will. I'll also surely have some regrets and certainly will apologize occasionally. There will be times where I'm confused, where I don't have the skills that would be helpful in a given situation. This is OK. It does not make me a bad person or inadequate.

My experience at the reception itself ran a full gamut. I enjoyed meeting alumnae and recalling times together at our Alma Mater; I felt uncomfortable in the outfit I wore and purse I carried; there was a broad range of conversation, international in flavor, including sharing and learning about a rich palette of diverse experiences; I judged others for their affluence and affectation; I appreciated the luxury of the hosts' home, their guests' contributions to literacy, the arts, the environment... And at times I actually felt quite comfortable and glad to be there, at that time, and to be me! In retrospect, I think that mom's struggles with insecurity pointed me toward valuable lessons.

At times I feel awkward in a situation, or do not have the information or skills needed. This is OK. I could even say I am not inadequate just because I might feel that way!

Had I known then what I am realizing today, I might have relaxed and breathed a little more deeply on the way to the reception. But I was just beginning the journey toward authenticity, even though the train had come to a full stop at the station in Bern, Switzerland and the host family was there to pick me up.

Related reading:

Dresser, Maureen (2005). *Multicultural Manners: Essential rules of etiquette for the 21st century.* Hoboken, NJ: John Wiley & Sons

Forni, P. M. (2002). *Choosing Civility: The twenty five rules of considerate conduct.* NY: St. Martin's Press

Harris, Thomas (1969). *I'm OK, You're OK.* NY: HarperCollins

Reflections: *In what situations have you felt, or do you still feel, insecure and uncomfortable? How do you cope with such situations today? What insights or strategies help you through such awkward or painful times? What does self-acceptance mean to you? And 'being yourself'? What factors help you to 'be yourself' at this stage in your life?*

*"Nothing has a stronger influence on
children than the unlived lives of their parents."* Carl Jung

"Only in solitude do we find ourselves." Miguel de Unamuno

୬୧

Being Alone

What does it all mean? Who am I? Why am I here? I have asked myself these questions at critical or difficult times in my life, as when a close relationship broke up or when I couldn't seem to find fulfilling work. At one of those times I started exploring my parents' lives. I became curious about issues that appeared to cause them unhappiness or difficulties. Pondering what seemed to me to be my parents' 'unfinished business' has provided some provocative ways of making sense of my own 'becoming.'

Consider my mom, Gerrie. At the age of 59, despite her vitality, her love of mothering, her health and financial security, two young grandchildren who adored her, and a baby granddaughter just nine months old, on Valentine's Day, she took her life. In her roles as mother, friend, creator, she was vitally alive. Her enthusiasm for nature and flower arranging affected the whole family. On a road trip we took when I was about ten she gasped and said, "Joe, stop the car. See those beautiful dried grasses and wildflowers? They'd be perfect for an arrangement I'm creating for the Garden Show." "Oh, look kids, here are some porcupine quills! Hop out and let's touch them!" But in that 59th year she had experienced a great loss. My dad had died of a sudden heart attack just eight months before. The note she left behind spoke of how 'inextricably intertwined' their lives had been.

While I respect and accept my mother's choice, I wondered what I could learn from her life, and I began to sift through my memories of her challenges.

It's true that she didn't manage her paperwork or financial affairs very well. After my dad's death she had spread out stacks of paper, checks, bills, over the entire dining room table. She was moving about the table anxiously, chilled white wine in hand, saying "I just don't know where to start. I find it overwhelming." But this didn't grab me as an issue that had significant implications for my life. Neither the alcohol, nor finances or paperwork. Yes, I'd had my frustrations with paper, and struggled with budgets at times. But mostly I have found that stacks of paper were an invitation to create order. So her overwhelm in this area was not 'unfinished business' that related to my life.

Smoking cigarettes heavily had been a nemesis for my mom. From 17 on, she spent her years relying on them for cold, tarry comfort, and was not able to stop despite numerous efforts and aims. But smoking had not been an issue for me either. Once as a sophomore in college, I decided to try to learn to smoke. It would give my hands something to do during those painfully awkward blind dates, and I also thought that it might help me lose weight. But after two days I thought better of it and stopped. These were clearly issues that caused my mother suffering, but that didn't slide into my life.

As I looked at the pieces of my mom's life and mine, pondering the notion of 'unfinished business,' I suddenly felt my heart start to beat harder, and my temples throb. The clutching and shortness of breath let me know I was getting close. There was something that my mom had not addressed successfully in her life that had a painful charge for me as well. She had been afraid, basically unable, to be on her own. She had lacked the inner resources to be alone. She did not have the courage or energy to continue her journey, even for a while, by herself.

It was just few months before she died that she told me about the dream I mentioned earlier, where she had walked into a social gathering and was completely ignored. Her voice had cracked as she told me, and at the time I thought she was being melodramatic, and didn't pay much attention. Later the dream and the fears it symbolized took on new significance. Visiting her after my dad's death, she said, almost under her breath, "I won't be a widow for long." While I didn't grasp the dire implications of what she may have meant that day, I did feel and share her distress at the thought of being on her own. This, then, was mom's unfinished business and my challenge as well.

With a jolt, I realized that for me too, the thought of being left out, alone, was terrifying—and had been from a very young age. Counselors in my elementary school had handed out a questionnaire that included the question: "What are you afraid of?" I had written in my childish printing "I wish I didn't have to be alone." Continuing through high school I agonized about inclusion and exclusion; I jumped into marriage straight from college; after 20 years I left my marriage and merged directly into another significant relationship. I was clearly avoiding being alone, at all costs. It was only in my forties that I began to come to grips with this fear, yes, terror, of being on my own.

True enough, we are social animals at core. We seek and need personal contact. Babies will not thrive without touch and love, and most of us prefer to be with a partner. A preference is one thing. Paralyzing fear is another.

For much of it, my life didn't seem complete unless I was with someone. I remember having a conversation with my sister-in-law about spending time alone. She told me she loved being alone! I found it hard to imagine when she told me she would often choose to go to a movie by herself, rather than have someone along. For me, any experience—watching a sunset, having a meal, seeing a movie—was improved by sharing it. I didn't value the experience nearly so much if it were just me, by myself. It seems to me now that this is because I didn't value myself.

Years later I was doing some research for a project. It was a spring afternoon in Southern California. The light was clear and luminous, the peonies in the garden of the Bed and Breakfast where I was staying were luscious, and my heart was singing. I was by myself, but I felt connected to my new partner, rapturously in love, and the world was alive and glistening for me. Things between us were 'right' at that moment.

Then we had a telephone conversation where some of the recurring doubt surfaced about his sense of our relationship working out. When I hung up the phone everything in my private universe was radically altered. My head was spinning, the world seemed menacing, and I felt isolated.

Objectively nothing had changed. I was in the garden of the B&B, the light, the peonies, the research—all were as before. But now I perceived myself to be alone. Or I feared I would be. I was all but paralyzed. I could hardly walk for a while. Even the realization that it was a perception, all internal, a future possibility and not a present reality, scarcely helped at the time. I still was devastated by the thought that I might be alone sometime in the future.

That was almost 20 years ago. I've danced a range of dances, journeyed various paths, been to different school houses and learned some of the lessons. I am finally coming to be more comfortable on my own, to enjoy time alone, to value watching a sunset as much when I am by myself as when there is someone beside me. It is my preference to be in a partnership, and I am. But the way I hold the possibility of being on my own, and the way I experience time on my own have transformed and softened. Inquiring into my mom's 'unfinished business' was an illumination of the way.

Related reading:

Almaas, A. H. (1986) *The Void: Inner spaciousness and ego structure.* Berkeley: Diamond Books

Chodron, Pema (1997). *When Things Fall Apart: Heart advice for difficult times.* Boston: Shambhala

Jeffers, Susan (1987). *Feel the Fear and Do It Anyway.* NY: Ballantine Books

Redfield, James (1993). *The Celestine Prophecy.* NY: Warner Books

Reflections: *What do you see as some aspects of your mother's 'unfinished business'? What might these areas mean for and to you? Select a particular area or issue where the impact on your life is challenging. Explore how you might like to address this issue in your life now, considering it unfinished business.*

"Only one koan matters: You." Chinese saying

We're all in this together—by ourselves." Lily Tomlin

Finding My Niche

As a young husband and dad, Joe Kremer decided to leave the deadening routine of a daily commute into the New York where he worked in the insurance business, as had his father. The move to Oklahoma, Indian Territory and the 'land of the red earth,' as my mom said, was a bold step. But in the 25 years my father lived and worked in the mid-west, he was, by his own admission, never happy or fulfilled. Although he brightened the lives of many people with his warm smile and friendly demeanor, and although he returned home from work each day whistling cheerfully, he harbored deep doubts about the meaningfulness of the work he'd done his entire professional life, about the quality of his friendships, and indeed his life in general.

Reflecting on our lives, it can be fruitful to look at both parents and their lifestyles. What did your father stand for? What were his strengths and accomplishments? What did he want from life that he never attained? What was he trying to establish in the world, regardless of how successfully?' Pondering these questions can help us with some of ours: Why am I here? What life issues are mine to address? Which are the areas to which I am invited to be sensitized?

My dad and I had a conversation one day. It is the only occasion I recall where my dad talked about his personal life, so it stands out in my memory. We were in the kitchen, and he was nursing his vodka tonic. I was doing homework, and he was looking over my shoulder. We began to talk about work. "I started out Pre-Med," he said in a flat tone. "And that didn't work. Couldn't stand the sight of blood. Tried working for my father. That was comfortable, but a dead end. Gerrie disapproved of it. She didn't even acknowledge when I got a raise, because she thought it was more like an allowance. It was very difficult. And now I've been working for years for someone else, and don't really care about the work. You know, Jill, I sometimes feel like I've wasted my life. What does it all mean? What's the point?" Years later, as I was experiencing similar feelings, I would love to have been able to talk again with my dad, but we never continued the conversation.

Mid-life my dad had taken a test with an outfit that assessed and evaluated aptitudes as a way of helping people make constructive decisions about school and work. He was trying to find work that was satisfying. But he returned home despondent after taking the test. The results indicated he was a man with 'too many aptitudes.' It's hard for such people to settle on a fulfilling area of work,' the evaluators had said.

Having a multitude of interests and talents was not a problem in and of itself. Indeed my dad enjoyed his broad range of interests. It was an ironic and harsh blow that my dad died of a sudden, massive heart attack when he was just 61. Only one month away from his retirement. For my mother it was devastating. She became a widow at a very young age. And for those close to my dad, it was heartbreaking because he had been feeling very optimistic about the new life he planned for himself in retirement. He would share a small office with a close business friend that would give him time away from home to look into business matters at his leisure. Now he was finally going to be able to enjoy and pursue his many interests. Playing the trumpet in a Dixieland band. Driving 'Meals on Wheels' to shut ins. Buying and fixing up a camper van for the travels he wanted to take with his wife and to visit his kids. He died without realizing any of these dreams of ease and balance in his life. He died feeling, to some degree, incomplete and discontent.

When my dad died I was 34, living in Europe, a young mom and wife. The earlier conversation with my dad haunted me as I came to see that, just like my dad, I never felt like I had a niche where I fit, and I was frequently discontent. I was busy, yes, and certainly had a niche as a mom and wife. In those days with two small children, house, husband, garden, dog and part time work, I was never without things to do. But I felt adrift, not only professionally, but culturally, emotionally, and spiritually as well.

The work that I was doing was opportunistic. It filled my time, served a purpose, kept my brain in gear, but it did not feel purposeful to me, nor was it where my heart and passion lay. I had put some energy into trying to find a direction that felt right for me, but to no avail. I wanted things to be different and was often critical of others and myself. It startled me greatly when I realized that this was also a characteristic of my dad's. This was a piece of my dad's 'unfinished business.' I had a flash of recognition as I saw how my dad's difficulties also described my own life up to that point.

Culturally, I was neither American any more, nor did I ever fully put down roots in Germany, where I lived for almost 20 years. It wasn't until I was moving away, at a farewell party that my German-American book club gave for me, that I realized I had actually resisted putting down roots, settling in. *The restless discontent and experience of not having a niche was largely inside!* My friends had been loyal and warm, but I had seen them as too different and not good enough. My work had been challenging and allowed me to travel and keep learning, but I was not satisfied. The list could go on, regarding family connections, activities, community… While there certainly are external factors that can contribute significantly to one's sense of ease and belonging, I was now recognizing and grappling with my own, personal internal restlessness and discontent, which were frequently present regardless of my external circumstances.

When I left my marriage and moved to Canada, I made a new start. I would do my best to finish what I saw as my father's unfinished business. I consciously opened to the willingness to accept a personal, professional and cultural niche. I made some vision drawings, which I still have today as a reminder.

The unfolding included acquiring citizenship, creating a home that was welcoming and beautiful, beginning to be part of a community, as well as finding work where I was contributing in ways that were meaningful to me. And indeed, it grew on me slowly but surely that through this process I was coming to feel that I had a niche, a sense of belonging at last. I was grateful and felt truly content in ways I think my dad had not been able to be. When I think of my dad I am reminded how we never know how much time we have left. How it is important not to put off making changes, internal as well as external, that we know inside will make a difference. Out of denial, fear or inertia.

Easier said than done. Yet intention can set a course.

Looking at our lives in the context of our parents', it's almost as though there is a momentum into which we are born, two points of view that we may choose to integrate into our journeys. We can also take this perspective to a spiritual dimension: our parents' lives can be seen as two approaches to life, with differences, and perhaps they are even contrary to each other. What if we have been placed here precisely to resolve and synthesize their truths into a higher form?

This perspective invites us to see our lives as a process through which one generation transforms the circumstances it inherits into other, more evolved and fuller forms. Our lives are a becoming; a process of understanding the combined truths of our families of origin, our early experiences, and then, gradually but ongoingly, inviting and co-creating the development and evolution. There's a way in which the telling of it becomes part of our mission. From this vantage point, we can see that the events, the synchronicities of our lives are part of this unfolding, this evolution, this mission. It is one way of enriching and inspiring the world.

Not long ago I was let go—fired, actually—from the team of trainers and conflict resolution work that had been profoundly fulfilling for me for almost 20 years. Yes, I could still do contract work, but the sense of community was altered and damaged. Shortly after this, the class that I had been teaching as a volunteer fitness instructor was cancelled. Yes, I could still substitute for other instructors and keep active. But the sense of belonging and being an important part of a team was changed, diminished. The diminishing of connection and contentment that came with the loss of a significant work and volunteer identity was challenging. My 'niche' that had been comfortable for the last decade was radically disrupted. It was profoundly disorienting.

Ah, change. There it was again. As I looked in the mirror at my middle-age face and body, and felt the familiar sense of who I had been and how I'd been functioning in the world falling away, it felt like a kind of death. But as I stayed with the experience I could sense it becoming rather like starting over. What would be my new niche, the new ways I would find my place? This time around I felt better equipped to face the gaps in my familiar and satisfying world.

I have heard a suggestion that it is good to re-invent oneself every ten years. I took a deep breath. It dawned on me that our 'business' in life is never really finished till it's over.

Related reading:

Cameron, Julia (1982). *The Artist's Way: A spiritual path to higher creativity.* NY: Penguin Putnam

Haidt, Jonathan (2006). *The Happiness Hypothesis: Finding modern truth in ancient wisdom.* NY: Basic Books

Redfield, James (1996). *The Tenth Insight: Holding the vision.* NY: Warner Books

Sheehy, Gail (1976). *Passages: Predictable crises of adult life.* NY: Bantam Books

Reflections: *What do you perceive as your father's unfinished business'? How have his choices affected your life? Taken together, how have both your parents' legacies affected you? To what degree have you chosen to address the issues that are relevant to your own life? If you find you have not done this, might it be fruitful to consider this investigation?*

"It is the supreme art of the teacher to awaken joy in creative expression and knowledge." Albert Einstein

"Think sideways!" Edward de Bono

This or That?

One fine fall afternoon several years ago I was taking a walk in Stanley Park with Oliver Hanson, a self-avowed SNAG (sensitive new age guy) with a warmth and eternal optimism that could leave even the biggest of pessimists feeling light and hopeful. Either that, or queasy and uncomfortable. I myself am often in sync with Oliver. I appreciate his broad smile, his out-of-the-box creativity and his commitment to a more just and healthy planet. It was Oliver who introduced me to the idea that people *or* situations are not this or that, but that they are rather this *and* that.

It was a startling idea from the outset. With the *or*, I am firmly rooted in the comparison mode. Either my grandmother was rigid *or* she was warm. It calls up judgment. Which is right, more accurate? When I make a choice, the feeling of closure is familiar and comfortable. 'Right. Got it. That's how she was. Ah, yes.' The *or* closes my curiosity right down. I am not asked to look at the situation more closely, explore the subtleties, to be open to discrepancies in my points of view. As French philosopher Simone Weil would have it, we stop looking. To be fully, deeply alive is to always keep looking, developing and giving attention. It is tempting, and often easier, to stop, but the consequences are harsh and limiting.

Becoming: Journeying toward Authenticity

Recognizing that my granny was rigid *and* warm helps me develop a more complete and differentiated understanding of her life and world. It dawned on me that my mother, too, was not insecure, mean-spirited *or* creative and nurturing. She was all this wrapped up into one: insecure, creative, mean, and nurturing, by turns.

When I can shift to the mode of this *and* that, I am more likely to see and appreciate complexities and ambiguities. When I accept the confusing and paradoxical implications of the *and*, I can shift from judgment to curiosity. And curiosity can beget compassion, a softening to others, and myself as well. The this *and* that mode invites open-endedness and scatters the autumn leaves, my stories – my fixed perceptions. Sometimes it even shakes my ways of making sense of things.

In the end, though, my stories are only the result of how I interpret and tell you about *my* experience of my mom and my granny. I wonder now about their own, personal experience of their lives. What were their joys, their trials and tribulations? What did they fear, what gave them strength? How did they experience their marriages, what was sex like? What disappointments and successes did they experience? What were their hopes and concerns for their children, for the world?

How delicious it would be to be able to sit down with them, savor a cup of hot tea or ice coffee together, to ask them questions, and, finally, to be able to listen with maturity, with curiosity and compassion, openness and acceptance, instead of the defending, comparing, evaluating that I so often brought to relationships. This won't happen. Both my mother and my grandmother have died. Yet I am the richer, softer and kinder for the curiosity, acceptance and compassion I can now feel for them both, for others and for myself.

Recognizing things are not this *or* that, and learning to hold the *and* instead, has helped me deal with many challenging situations and paradoxes with curiosity and acceptance.

One common spiritual image is that of God (or god, goddess, or the mystery, the absolute... there are many terms from which to choose, if you choose), as an ocean and individuals as separate waves. When I am stuck in the belief of this *or* that, the sense that I'm a wave differentiates and separates me in some way from the whole ocean. This distinctness and individuality might have a flavor of pumped-up power to it, but that is a false grandiosity. The single wave is isolated, cold, alone, to crash on a shore and be gone forever. It's barren and harsh, disconnected to the ebb and flow of life.

Then I step back and realize that perhaps I am the wave *and* the ocean, I am both unique, distinct, individual—no other wave is in this place at this time, with these qualities—yet I am also inseparably connected to the ocean. Some suggest, using a holographic or mystical view, that we actually *are* the ocean. Whether I am, or am part of, the ocean, I feel grounded, connected, held—integrally and indivisibly conjoined to something larger than myself. I am nourished by and included in the beauty of the whole, even as I enjoy my uniqueness and particularity.

Related reading:
Bolen, Jean (2001). *Goddesses in Older Women: Archetypes in women over fifty.* NY: HarperCollins
Meyers, Linda (2007). *Becoming Whole: Writing your healing story.* Berkeley: Two Bridges Press
Murdock, Maureen (1990). *The Heroine's Journey: Woman's quest for wholeness.* Boston: Shambhala
Weil, Simone (2001). *Waiting for God.* NY: HarperCollins

Reflections: *Think of a person in your life whom you have 'boxed in' by neglecting to realize they are this and that? What happens if you change your perception from or to and regarding this person? Think of a situation where you created an or where an and would have worked as well or better? What would you gain and/or what would you give up if you transformed your perspective?*

"I embrace emerging experience. I participate in discovery. I am a butterfly. I am not a butterfly collector." William Stafford

"Infinitely more important than the answers are the questions, the choice of them, the inner form of them." Oswald Spengler

༄

Metaphors and Worldviews

Related reading:
Adyashanti (2000). *The Impact of Awakening.* Los Gatos, CA: Open Gate Publishing
Maitri, Sandra (2006). *The Spiritual Dimension of the Enneagram: Nine faces of the soul.* NY: Penguin
Schaef, Anne Wilson (1992). *Women's Reality: An emerging female system in a white male society.* NY: HarperCollins
Tulku, Tarthang (1977). *Time, Space, and Knowledge: A new vision of reality.* Emeryville, CA: Dharma Publishing
Wilber, Ken (2000). *A Theory of Everything: An integral vision for business, politics, science, and spirituality.* Boston: Shambhala

"The most beautiful thing we can experience is the mysterious…who can no longer pause to wonder and stand rapt in awe, is as good as dead." Albert Einstein

"Without leaving my house, I know the whole universe." Lau-Tsu

◈

Safe and Mysterious

…describes one way I often experience my world. I think it's in part because of the time I spent as a child with my father's mother. I called her Granny. She was quiet spoken yet substantial, of German extraction and southern upbringing. An unlikely but intriguing combination. She was solid, round and warm, slow-moving and gentle, her waist-long gray hair, wrapped and twisted around her head, crowning her face like a dilapidated tiara.

Granny's scent was not the mildly objectionable mustiness of an older person; she smelled sweet and kind, a scent that veritably urged me to cuddle in as close as I could. The house itself had perhaps a slight moldy smell, but it was tantalizingly mixed with the scent of Jergen's hand lotion. That almond aroma also permeated the air in the guest bedroom of Granny's summer house, where she always had the beds made up and ready for us, just in case…The almondness of the lotion reminds me even today of my granny's healing feeling.

Then there was the fragrance of freshly baked chocolate chip cookies that Nellie, Granny's crisp and competent Irish Catholic maid, had made. I could have as many of those cookies as I wanted, whenever I wanted, and the kitchen pantry where I went to get them was clean and bright, inviting, open, and there was no one who ever said 'No,' or 'That's enough, Jill.' There was a sense of 'It's OK, I'm OK, the world is light and luscious' that wafted off those cookies and out of that kitchen. Sometimes I'd eat them sitting in my granny's lap. She never counted.

She wore those 'old lady' dresses, made of printed, flimsy material which sort of clung and draped, belted at the waist, which really wasn't much of a waist on Granny, because she had a substantial body. Her waist was just the center of the barrel that was her middle. She sat in a rocking chair, and presided. It was clear that no danger could arise as long as Granny was rocking. Leaning back in that chair, smiling in an accepting, knowing kind of way, she would frequently say "Merceeàwnuss." Her gentle commentary on things. It was only in my fifties that I realized Granny must have been saying "Mercy on us!" and I would love to have asked her what she actually meant! To me it always meant, 'Well, here we are, and everything's gonna be alright.'

And indeed, in this life, one might say "Merceeàwnuss" now and then, or "Goodness be" or "Oh my," and not know exactly what was coming next. And in Granny's world there certainly were some things for which one definitely needed to be on the lookout. Black cats were to be assiduously avoided, and leaning ladders, and number thirteens. But hanging out with Granny, and being in her house, as a pre-schooler and even a teenager, I learned that, by and large, the world was a safe place. Full of intriguing sights, enchanting smells and unexpected adventure. A place to revel in and savor.

Listening to Granny tell stories about her life was like being invited aboard a magic carpet. You never knew where you'd be going. Perhaps to the fields of the plantation on which she grew up, along on the trips she took with her two sisters, remembering the Easter egg hunts on the grand lawn. Once, with a wistful smile, her eyes focused in the distance, she told me of a trip she and her husband, Bern had taken, and how he always said she had the brownest eyes he'd ever seen. She rested sweetly in that contentment, and I received that amicable kindheartedness by osmosis. To me, her eyes did not really look brown. They were that kind of gray-green-yellow-brown of older people's eyes. But no matter the color, there was something hard to put a finger on, yet unmistakably present in Granny's eyes that let me feel the confidence and ease you have when someone is loved and loves you.

She gave me her full and undivided attention, which is, lamentably, not something children often receive from adults. She didn't count the cookies I ate, but to Granny I counted. We played Canasta by the hour, for as long as I wanted, building up huge piles, and getting excited together about who, in the end, would finally be able to take the big pile and add substantially to their score. Somehow it didn't matter who won, we were in it together.

On special days she'd take me along with her to her inside garden. "Jill, sweet, come along with me." I think it's properly called a winter garden, but to me it was the room with green, moist, layers of plants, blooming, light, and exotic; palpable, humid air, and sunshine reflecting through layers and angles of hot house glass on to the vibrant magenta, crimson and dark violet of Granny's gloxinias. Mercy on us, Granny was proud of her gloxinias. The pleasure she took in them was infectious.

When I was about three or four, my Granny took me by the hand, and we walked into the dark front entry hall of her grand, old, three story stucco house, where the grandfather clock chimed the hours with its rich, deep gong. Granny leaned over close to me and said in a whisper, "Now Jill, don't you be afraid of the clock." From that moment on, I was terrified to come near the clock or to even go into the hall without Granny. But that didn't mean I loved her any less.

My mother did though. Love her less. My Granny enjoyed, to my mother's dismay, eating large quantities of thick, rich, delicious cream, cookies and other treats. She had no trouble whatsoever polishing off a pint of ice-cream in one sitting. I loved her for the treats. My mother, thin, fit, and image-conscious, disapproved of these indulgences. My dad worshipped her. His devotion to her was rooted, at least in part, in her unstoppable dedication when he had been seriously ill as a young child. They were very close and regularly had long conversations.

These conversations, and this relationship, lay like a cold and wet blanket over my parents' marriage. One Thanksgiving dinner, my mother had worked hard to prepare the traditional, perfect, turkey-with-all-the-fixin's dinner. We had just sat down when the phone rang. It was Granny. My dad answered the phone and talked with her, as always, at his leisure and for a very long time. Dinner grew cold and colder. My mother's stomach churned until she finally left the table and threw up.

As a child I knew nothing of these ambiguities and subtleties, dynamics and shadow sides. Mothers and grandmothers of that generation had their own particular limitations and maternal values, born or bred of their nature and their 19th century Victorian up bringing which blended uniquely with their kind, nurturing qualities. And who are we to judge, saint or shadow, praise or blame? No point in that.

What I do know is that in my particular case, I learned by being in Granny's company that the world is a safe and scrumptious place, a kaleidoscope of sights and flavors, smells and sounds, experiences to savor and absorb. As I reflect today on my early experience, I discern that learning also about the occasional ominous grandfather's clock, black cat or leaning ladder contributed not so much a sense of fear or anxiety, but rather added a feeling of mystery, excitement, wonder to the mix.

Safe and full of mystery: isn't this how a number of spiritual teachings point to the nature of reality? Safe from the ravages of time, eternal, deep and unfathomable. Who would have guessed that eating cookies on Granny's lap, I was, in a way, probing and absorbing the essential nature of all that is!

Related reading:

Bolen, Jean (2001). *Goddesses in Older Women: Archetypes in women over fifty.* NY HarperCollins

Miles, Rosalind (1988). *The Women's History of the World.* London: Paladin Grafton Books

Schaefer, Carol (2006). *Grandmothers Counsel the World: Women elders offer their vision for our planet.* Boston: Shambhala

Sheilds, Carol, Marjorie Anderson, eds. (2003). *Dropped Threads 2: More of what we aren't told.* Toronto, ON: Vintage Canada

Reflections: *Who, besides your parents, had a significant influence on you in your childhood? What did you learn about the world from these people? What was the nature, what were the aspects, of these influences? How do they affect you today? What are you passing on to younger people about the nature of the world?*

"Each one of you is perfect as you are. And you all could use a little bit of improvement." Shunryu Suzuki

"The world is not to be put in order, the world is order incarnate. It is for us to put ourselves in unison with this order." Henry Miller

Universe Unfolding

'The universe is unfolding just as it should, things are perfect just as they are.' On hearing these phrases my first reaction can be: 'Are you kidding me? Not only are things not perfect, there is a huge mess of circumstances that are horrible: the pollution, destruction, despoiling and looting of the environment; global warming and the disasters resulting from climate change; the decimation and disappearance of species, languages, cultures, eviscerated by the raw, western, industrial, materialistic, capitalistic way of life; exploding and exponential population growth; starvation, exploitation, corruption, greed, war, famine... And this list is a bare bones beginning.'

Notwithstanding my initial gut reactions to the contrary, there are voices from many quarters proclaiming that indeed the universe is perfect.

What are we to make of these voices?

There are days when I am sublimely aligned with the perfection: I see how winter frost transforms the fall leaves into lace; or a drop of dew flashes rainbows refracted by sunlight; I am touched to the point of tearing up, (and my grandson will say to me again "Grandma, are your eyes watering?") at the magnificence and variety of creation and its inhabitants, the utter abundance of intricate shapes and forms, and yes, I marvel even at us humans.

I have no trouble believing, or better yet, I find it hard *not* to believe in a deeper force, a profound source before and beyond space and time.

Since we can't google the answer, and there are there are no ultimate references, only ongoing debates on whether there is a god, a beneficent prime mover, a mystical first cause, let's, for curiosity's sake, see where the juxtaposition of the two views might lead us: say we accept the perfection of creation, (or at least don't reject this possibility out of hand), and also observe the alarming signs of distress obvious to any casual observer of our planet.

One possibility that could result from 'accepting things as they are' is that one might resign and sit on one's duff, attributing everything to chance, karma, predestination or the astrological alignment (one's own, or that of the times), or the numerological phase currently holding sway, and become entirely passive.

If we focus on the world as a mess, we might feel called upon to spend every waking hour doing what we can, feel the responsibility to 'fix it,' make it better, make a difference, take charge, serve, lighten the load, try harder—and because situations seem to be getting worse, we've got to run even harder... When I am in this mode, I can feel the push, the agitation, the hope, the drive, the burden, the call, the onerous cloak of responsibility. This approach to the world situation, and even to small sections of our lives, can create ulcers or migraines. Worse, acting from this place, we may be under the illusion that *we* are the prime movers, the doers, the ones in charge, leading to a disconnected grandiosity and the probable crash of hubris.

Interestingly, the responses could almost be reversed as well: the world's a mess, but it's karma or chance and there's nothing I can do; the world is perfection manifesting and I'm part of the groovy flow, blithely ignoring the messes. Either way the dilemma is sliced, it seems fraught with paradox and contradiction.

But the lack of answers or accessible solutions doesn't mean the questions go away. What are we to make of these widely

Becoming: Journeying toward Authenticity

expressed, yet seemingly contradictory views? Regardless of how we respond to the views, we are still left with two contradictory approaches. Either the world *is* perfect and unfolding in an optimal way *or* it's in a near hopeless mess and we need to do something about it.

Or maybe, just maybe, it's not this *or* that which is appropriate here; it could be this *and* that. What might come of conjoining the two perspectives?

Simultaneously with the teaching of the perfection of creation, numerous spiritual teachers have elucidated the perspective that we must live in the present moment and accept what is. These are said to be key components and markers of inner peace and psychic ease. Upset again at the dilemma I felt when I thought of all that seems unjust, inequitable, or disintegrating, I was greatly relieved when one of my teachers pointed out that *accepting* need and does not mean *condoning*.

Maybe this is a path through the wormhole—one way to reconcile the paradox, to join the two disparate approaches: The universe is unfolding as it should, *and* we need a project.

Accepting yet not condoning aligns me again with appropriate action: I can, and indeed, am called to act. Find a project, choose my action. Not listlessly, or motivated by hate or fear, but with an open heart, out of love and with full-on passion. Johanna Macy, for example, is a contemporary disciple of Buddhism, a teaching in which acceptance and equanimity are core tenets. Johanna talks passionately about turning from the industrial growth society to a life-sustaining civilization. She urges and encourages people today to find the courage to act, despite rapidly worsening conditions; *to accept but not condone.* Acknowledge what is, and tackle a project.

This blend of acceptance and action can apply in transformative ways for young people as well. There are plenty of dictums and circumstances that children have to accept: that they must brush their teeth, wash hands after peeing, go to bed when they'd like to play; parents don't always listen or understand them, friends aren't always loyal or trustworthy. In this world of contradiction and excess, one of the best things a parent can do for a child's self-esteem is to find and support an activity at which the child can excel. And help them to hold seemingly incompatible emotions and situations simultaneously. Here we have it again: *Accept what is, and embrace a project.* It is also said that excelling at an activity encourages joy and contribution, and goes far to helping kids resist peer pressure when it's tough. And healing for us adults as well!

When we do good works, we must let go of the outcome. This is part of acceptance. Not easy. Sometimes harder than the task itself. Our egos want to co-opt our efforts, want to take credit, take us out of alignment with a larger flow. We need to do our work, engage in our chosen projects regardless of the possibility of success, in some cases because it's the right thing to do, it's where we are called to be.

Even when there is no perceptible progress or evident achievement, our efforts per se can be handsomely rewarding. A number of activists, spiritual warriors, engaging passionately for people and the planet, have exhorted us not to engage holding the expectation of triumph, ultimate victory of good over evil, or even clear, steady progress. They suggest that being a part of a movement of growing consciousness, unfolding, with the fits and starts of small successes along with obvious and painful defeats, bringing patience and persistence to the process—this all is worthwhile. The very involvement with just causes and committed people is satisfying, inspiring, and deeply pleasurable.

When, on felicitous days, I can both experience sumptuousness and majesty of the universe (or simply the flower on my balcony), and also find the blend of acceptance and action in the projects that engage me, I am uplifted and grounded at the same time. I'm uplifted by appreciation and wonder, grateful to be alive, and simultaneously grounded; my feet are planted firmly and I'm rooted in the task at hand. Things are perfect *and* I've got a project.

Becoming: Journeying toward Authenticity

Related Reading:

Almaas, A. H. (2008). *The Unfolding Now: Realizing your true nature through the practice of presence.* Boston: Shambhala

Macy, Johanna (1991). *World As Lover, World As Self: Courage for global justice and ecological renewal.* Berkeley: Parallax Press

Sanguin, Bruce (2007). *Darwin, Divinity, and the Dance of the Cosmos.* Kelowna, BC: Wood Lake Publishing

Swimme, Brian and Thomas Berry ((1992). *The Universe Story.* NY: HarperCollins

Zinn, Howard (2002). *The Power of Nonviolence: Writings by advocates of peace.* Boston: Beacon Press

Reflections: *Where and when, if at all, do you experience the perfection of the universe? How do you feel about turmoil on the planet? What do you believe about the intersection of the two? What happens as you try to consider both simultaneously? What are your 'projects' at the present time?*

*"Wherever we go, whatever we do, self is the sole
subject we study and learn."* Ralph Waldo Emerson

*"Life is the real teacher and the
Curriculum is all set up."* Larry Rosenberg

൧ඁ

Living Lessons

My first school was close to home, in the small New Jersey town where I grew up. Only a few blocks away. Most days I walked with a friend, and when school started in the fall, we kicked leaves and gathered chestnuts for Show and Tell. I felt safe coming and going, adored my teachers and loved being in class. High school had its elevated moments as well, intertwined with the painful lessons of the effects of judgment and exclusion, conforming, efforting. At university, a venerable institution, complete with ivy-covered walls, a wide variety of courses were offered, and the instructors were first rate.

These influential educational experiences have led me, at times, to see life as one extensive, experiential school. In this school of lifelong learning, lessons are offered on a rolling schedule, all year long, and may begin any time day or night, not limited to weekdays between 8:30 and 3:00.

If life is a school, who, then, are the teachers? My personal answer to this question has emerged over the years, like a figure taking shape little by little, as it looms out of the fog on a misty morning, coming closer and closer. But the outline seems quite clear to me now. I always liked outlines. They give the overview, that shape of things, and one needn't attend to every detail. For me the big picture is clear: there is a higher power that transcends our everyday comings and goings, that is the source of everything, that was there before there was anything. I am inclined to refer to it as Being, or the mystery, sometimes god or goddess, God... Perhaps the teachers are manifestations of this power, or maybe the power itself is the teacher, manifesting in manifold ways.

In the end it doesn't really matter to me, which is just as well, because there are no definitive answers. Each person finds his or her own personal syllabus. What I find instructive about this metaphor, though, are the implications and possibilities of lifelong learning. One never knows when or where a new lesson might appear unexpectedly, or be presented very explicitly, by whom or in what form.

On good days, I find this exhilarating, just as I found the beginning of a new school year to be. There were new, sharp pencils; crisp, fresh paper; the pungent smell of the leather school bag; a lunch box with a handle and a special treat; usually some new clothes for the first day of school. It was a memorable occasion, the start of a new adventure and expanded horizons. Usually I was ready for the new and could hardly wait. Sometimes it seems as if this higher power seems to 'know' exactly when to offer a particular 'class' or lesson.

There are, of course, times when I am not open or interested, or able to understand what is being presented. And if I am not ready the first time, or second, my experience has been that the universe keeps offering me the same lesson again until I am able to finally absorb the learning, until I finally 'get it.' A lesson of this sort may be called an AFGO. (Another Frigging Growth Opportunity.)

Here's an example of a repeating lesson in my life. It just kept showing up, presenting itself, being presented. I kept resisting, looking the other way. To no avail. It didn't go away until I addressed it head on. This process wasn't exactly uplifting. But gripping, breath-taking, spine-tingling? Yes. It has to do with my experience of aloneness.

As an infant and a first child, I was frequently left alone, in my playpen or crib, sometimes to cry myself to sleep, never mind what my body needed or soul wanted. I'm sure my mom meant well. She may even have ached hearing the cries, but she was a product of her age and the prevailing child-raising norms, according to which a child would get spoiled if you picked her up every time she cried. Unless the baby was wet or hungry, you were supposed to leave the baby alone when it was time to sleep and she'd fall asleep before long. And fall asleep, I probably did, but I also imbibed the experience of being left alone. It impressed my soul, embedded itself deeply in the unconscious fabric of my being: people will sometimes leave you alone, and it can be very painful and scary.

As I grew up, and well into my mature decades, I was afraid of being alone. Actually terrified. I avoided any extended solitary period at all costs. Even though I had friends and contacts, the fear of being alone, or ending up alone, was visceral: I could feel the hole in my gut, the stringy tentacles of the fear spreading out into my arms and legs. I did whatever I could to avoid being with this feeling: I ate, I exercised, I talked on the phone, I checked my e-mail, I worked ... I had a creative set of distractions to avoid facing my fear.

I'm not suggesting there was anything seriously wrong with these strategies. They worked and were the best I could manage at the time. Nor am I judging the behaviors as inappropriate. What I later noticed, though, is that these coping strategies were largely defenses I used to protect myself from acknowledging and dealing with the fear head on. I wasn't ready to hear the lesson or look into the possibility of the learning, the growth and change that can occur when we stay with our experience instead of trying to escape from it. I had no interest or capacity for many years.

It was only after deciding to leave my first marriage that I finally spent some time alone, living by myself.

I had basically gone from my family home straight to university, from university to marriage, and after divorce, right into a second relationship. Then there was a gap. I had separated from my second life partner, and was now, finally, inexorably, undeniably, by myself, alone. I was in my fifties, and actually on my own for the first time. It was very much like taking a new course. On Your Own, 101. And while it may have been fairly basic, it felt more like an upper level graduate course to me, and one that I was very ill prepared for, having assiduously avoided the intro level opportunities. How anyone could say they actually preferred doing something alone was a mystery to me.

As I look back, I'd say that learning to be alone was about learning to value myself, to trust and appreciate my own experience. This ultimately would be the deeper level realization, the transformation that would take me beyond my coping strategies. But I still had stacks of required reading and a big pile of homework to do.

When, in my fifties, for the first time, I finally began to acknowledge, really feel and accept the fear of being alone, it started to lose its power over me. I remember sitting on a comfortable sofa in front of a crackling fire. It was dark outside. I was alone and I was afraid. For the first time in my life, I decided to consciously feel the fear. I noticed where it was in my body. In my gut. Spherelike. Soft edges. A kind of a grey blob, dense but not hard. Then emptiness.

When the time came that I was finally able to grapple with my fear, it began to dissipate, as if by magic. When I simply stayed with the experience instead of fleeing it, it actually became kind of interesting. It didn't kill me. It didn't even really hurt. I began to journal, to describe what was unfolding. And the experience began to change. I wrote, "the fear begins to fade and I begin to feel adequate, present in the moment. I have a knowingness that I am, that I'll be OK, that I can handle, benefit from, be open to, whatever comes." The darkness became a soft blanket that embraced and held me. The fire warmed me; the flickering on the wall delighted me. I made a cup of tea and settled in. I began to enjoy my own experience, just me, just there, just then.

I have felt the fear again, but I had begun to learn the lesson, and the fear is not the same. The panic does not paralyze. It brings me to the present moment. I am enough.

When I was first on my own, one of my anxieties was regarding what would happen if I got sick by myself, all alone. Who would care for me? How bad would it be? How would I manage? Perhaps I was ready for the next chapter in the lesson on being alone, because promptly after my partner and I parted ways, I came down with a real case of the flu. And somewhat to my surprise, I managed just fine! I made tea, cuddled in bed, turned up the heat and paid attention. This too passed, and the anxiety dissipated. After all, I could go to a doctor if needed, or call a friend or neighbor. I learned, when I was ready, that I could handle not only being on my own, but also being sick by myself.

There are times when I experience a certain excitement when I'm in a new situation: What will it be like? How will I do in this class? Will what I've mastered so far see me through the new experience? Ultimately, will I take the opportunity for learning and growth that life is offering in this situation? Can I take the learning to a deeper level?

And there are times when I dread the new situation. Is this an AFGO? The same questions may occur: What will it be like? How will I do? Will what I've mastered so far see me through? Will I step into the opportunity for learning? The excitement may be tinged with concern.

No matter. If I don't recognize and comprehend the essence this time, I'll always get another chance!

Related reading:

Albom, Mitch (1997). *Tuesdays with Morrie: An old man, a young man, and life's greatest lesson.* NY: Broadway Books

Blackmore, Susan (1999). *The Meme Machine.* Oxford: Oxford University Press

Wilber, Ken (1996). *A Brief History of Everything.* Boston: Shambhala

Wolff, Robert and Thom Hartmann (2001). *Original Wisdom: Stories of an ancient way of knowing.* Rochester, Vermont: Inner Traditions

Reflections: *In what ways does your life seem like an institution of learning, (higher or lower)? What is a lesson you think you've (more or less) mastered? Name one that seems to be offered again and again? Where does the metaphor break apart and what, if anything, can be inferred from the shards?*

*"There's a crack in everything: that's
how the light gets in."* Leonard Cohen

*"I think we all have a core that's ecstatic, that knows and that looks
up in wonder. We all know that there are marvelous moments of eternity that just
happen. We know them."* Coleman Barks

ⱱↄↄ

Shall We Dance?

L
ife for me is, on good days, a wild and gently rhythmic dance.
Moreover, I believe we are danced by life and are not, as we
often pridefully assume, the directors of the dance.

I haven't always seen it this way. One evening, over twenty
years ago, it was getting dark as I was driving home from a
workshop with Robert, an acquaintance and fellow student. That
drive became a turning point in my life.

The sky was ragged—wild, gusty winds were shoving ominous,
black clouds across the heavens, matching my state of mind. I was
talking about my relationship, the communication challenges, the
misunderstandings, the hurt. Robert was driving, and without
even turning to look at me, said, "You see life as a struggle, don't
you, Jill."

We had just completed a personal growth workshop, which
was, in Germany at that time, a fringe event. Workshops like that
one had begun to shift and rupture the supporting beams of the
psychological house I'd lived in for my 40 some years, but the
foundations were still quite firm.

Robert's words startled me, and I realized that yes, of course,
that was often the way I saw and experienced difficult times, and
more generally, life itself: as a struggle, a battle, a fight. It seemed
obvious to me, and I had never questioned it. Life as a struggle

Becoming: Journeying toward Authenticity

implied working hard, trying your best to survive, to come out on top.

These values inculcated in my childhood were incorporated into my psyche. My mind churns recalling the familiar anxiety associated with this life-as-struggle metaphor. Always wondering whether I'm doing it right, torn by the confusion and discomfort I felt living with ambiguities. It seems now like hopping on one foot then the other, struggling to avoid feeling the coals of fear beneath my feet. And up until then, I knew no alternative.

So when Robert said, "You can also experience life as a dance, you know, Jill," something cracked, and through the fracture I could see a pale light.

I love to dance. I love choreography and new steps, I take pleasure in following the lead of a stranger, being swept up, grooving to the music. I have rhythm in my flesh and blood and it started early. When I was a child, my brother and I drifted off to sleep every night to the sounds of my dad playing the piano in the living room as his special goodnight gift to my brother Jamie and me. He played an array of tunes, from *Johnny Comes Marching Home Again!* to *Clair de Lune*.

As the years went by he added modern tunes as well, *The Girl from Ipanema*, then *Indian Lake is a Scene You Should Make*. My brother, now called Jim, no longer Jamie, had just moved to Indian Lake, RI, and dad was delighted there was even a song extolling its virtues: *"Indian Lake is a scene you should make with your little one, Keep it in mind ..."* The rhythms and the words infused me.

And then he'd always play my very favorite, a piece whose melody and lyrics both give me goose bumps to this day: *Nature Boy*: *"The greatest thing you'll ever learn...Is just to love and be loved in return."*

When I experience life as a dance I feel fluid, I smile, I move, I delight. The tough times can be danced too, maybe even celebrated. But I had to learn this. First I struggled. And the dance can feel much like a struggle when I'm stuck in the past. I remember a time when my husband and I had gotten crunchy with each other; he was not talking, had gone to bed. I was hurt, sad and wanted desperately to sort it out. We'd learned very different rhythms and steps! The patterns I had learned involved engaging, hanging in there, trying to understand and get in sync with each other. He had learned to take a time out, step back, sit one out. He found that the safer way to go.

It felt like a new dance for us both when we tried something completely fresh: In an inspired moment I said "How long are you going to be mad at me this time?" "Six days, one hour and fifty minutes," he said, and we both started to giggle. We weren't struggling any more. We had broken out of the old moves into a new dance.

Contradancing is a form of country dancing that has been around for centuries. If you ever danced the Virginia Reel in elementary school, that's an example of contradancing. You and your partner are in line with other couples. Choosing partners is gender neutral. Boys ask girls, women ask men. You dance same sex if the numbers don't come out even. It's all mix and match, like life can be. You never refuse someone a dance unless you need to sit the dance out from sheer exhaustion. The movements are taught fresh each dance, each moment new. This is a core spiritual teaching. Yup, it's all we have, the present moment. Be here, now. Not thinking or believing we've got it down, not being so grandiose as to think we know what's coming, but being open to what might emerge. It could be a do-si-do your neighbor, a swing your partner, or pass though and greet the new.

In Contradancing, the dance dances you. The fiddles and banjos start their compelling rhythms, and my body starts to move with the beat. The caller starts to call and the floor comes alive, hundreds of bodies turning, faces smiling, swinging, flowing. Without knowing exactly how, just moving with the music and paying attention to the caller, being present, I'm moving down the line, with my partner, dancing with couple after couple. It is warm and unabashed, a safe and respectful sensual thrill. The dance dances me.

Driving home with Robert that day, it was still dark, and would get darker: a healthy relationship, work that I embraced and experienced as contribution were still not on the horizon. Finally letting down roots and feeling I belonged, dancing with abandon and delight, would all be a long time coming. But there was a golden sliver of luminosity on the horizon that evening in Germany: life can be experienced as a dance, rather than a struggle.

Light was dawning. Shall we dance?

Related reading:
Castenada, Carlos (1969). *The Teachings of Don Juan: A Yaqui way of knowledge.* Berkeley: University of California Press
Eisler, Riane and David Loye (1998). *The Partnership Way: New tools for living and learning.* NY: HarperCollins
Taylor, Jill Bolte (2008). *My Stroke of Insight.* NY: Riverhead Books

Reflections: *Think of a time when you have experienced life as a struggle, as something to be overcome? What effect does this have on you? Think of one or two other metaphors for your life. Consider two specific experiences that have been pivotal for you. How do they each get represented in the metaphors? What doors could the metaphors open in the way you regard these experiences?*

"If you don't find God in the next person you meet, it's a waste of time looking for him further." Mohandas K. Gandhi

"There is a garden in every childhood, an enchanted place where colors are brighter, the air softer, and the morning more fragrant than ever again." Elizabeth Lawrence

Gardens and Gifts

There are many kinds of gardens in our lives, not just the ones that grow flowers or vegetables. One could think of a circle of friends as a kind of garden, the arrangement of our cupboards, the plates and herbs we choose, the range of jobs we've held…

The life of an octogenarian Austrian great-grandma I knew comprised several kinds of gardens. Considering Oma's variety of gardens has helped me reflect on mine. I have found the metaphor of life itself as a garden to be fruitful (pun intended) and munificent.

Oma has a vital and robust will to live, even under her present challenging circumstances. She is in her nineties now, frail, confused, wizened, but her face can shine like a fading flower's last bloom as, with her sense of humor and unrelenting determination, she determines to makes the best of the situation.

She has given richly to life and her gardens and received bounty in return. Oma spent much of her working life in schools, where she was beloved, and known as strict and fair, by the countless children she taught in elementary school, in the same village where she lived for some 75 years. She loved her children, telling about the scraggly ones, the bright ones, the quiet ones. As adults they'd stop by her home to bring a token of their lasting affection and admiration: a dozen eggs their chickens had laid, some mountain meadow honey from their dad's beehives, a piece of freshly smoked meat. These students, young and older, were clearly like a garden for her. She appreciated their many different varieties: each one unique and with a particular charm, fragrance and contribution to the panoply.

Oma's backyard was the regular kind of growing garden. I see her bending over the vegetables to choose some for soup, or summoning the children and grandchildren with, "The currants are ripe now. Come help pick them and we'll make a cake." She cared for her growing garden with dedication. There were the pear and walnut trees, the currant bushes, red and black. The beds of herbs and leeks and carrots, and the luscious, deep purple clematis that exploded in springtime on the trellis around the back yard terrace. Oma had a compost pile before that was the 'green' thing to do, making rich soil for her garden from the waste of her kitchen. Things cycled and flowed, gave forth and multiplied. Fruits and vegetables, flowers, and weeds.

I remember the many times I visited her, sat in her kitchen or helped in the garden. She was always the chief cook, always the master gardener. She was generous, industrious, typically busy preparing food, and welcoming her children and grandchildren. I remember the many times I shelled and ground the walnuts from the tree in the front yard for a delicious 'Potitze' (coffee cake), or beat the egg whites by hand with a whisk in a brass bowl, because that way they would get lighter and more voluminous than when beaten by a mixer. And as we sat in the kitchen together, working side by side, we talked about life, love, hardships, challenges, and values. Oma believed that many aspects of life were to be tended, cared for, and she manifested this belief in numerous ways. Her garden was a living example.

Friendships were another. Friendships, like flowers, Oma implied, beautify our lives, they need to be watered and cultivated. "I don't want to be alone in my old age," Oma said. "I want and need friends, and friendships don't just happen. I try to call my friends up regularly, and keep in touch. And I'm always interested in meeting new people." She then described a couple in her village she had known for a long time. "Edith," she said, "was no saint, and Fred was a bit hard to take sometimes too, had a way of needing always to be right. But I've known them so long, we've been through tough times together. They've stood by me and I by them, and that's what real friendship is about."

Some people say that plants respond when we talk to them. Oma talked to Edith and Fred, as well as her other friends, regularly. She set up times for a coffee klatsch or an outing together. She didn't wait for others to get in touch. Or sit and pout if there had been a long gap of silence. She picked up the phone, like a hoe. She was pro-active and intentional. And she nurtured a large circle of friends, young and old, from all walks of life, who continue to visit her now, in her fragile old age.

Oma was pretty good at accepting folks as they were, blemishes along with the blossoms. Yet the picture is not only pretty. Oma, along with the best and rest of us, could complain about people's shortcomings. Yes, she saw, and commented, that Fred had his curmudgeonly side, and she was prone to take perceived familial slights personally. But Fred was her friend nevertheless and she cherished him and the friendship. Her approach of cultivating life and friends, having fun and continuing to learn, became a model for me. The metaphor of life-as-a-garden was a radical contrast to the life-as-a-struggle that had been with me unconsciously since early on, periodically leaking into my psyche and my approach to friends, work, and marriage.

In addition to her ability to be accepting of fate and friends, Oma could be fiercely determined. She negotiated skillfully to acquire milk for her small children born during the bleak and frighteningly uncertain war years; she stayed up all night knitting little sweaters from used or salvaged yarn, so that her kids could be warm. And I think family members would all agree that she was downright stubborn at times, especially when crossed.

Stubborn and hard to dislodge. Like some weeds! It was not easy or smart to have a perspective that differed from hers. Her usual first response to any new idea was an emphatic 'No.' Even if she agreed in principle or came around to a compromise, the conversation invariably started with 'No.'

She needed to be the first and final authority too. She had been a teacher in school, and she was an authority in her garden. I remember one time when I was on my way to Graz, the cultural center in southeastern Austria near the village where Oma lived. I didn't need advice on when to go or how to get there. I was in my fifties and had made the trip countless times. But she told me to go here, there, take this bus, don't take this turn, watch out for that... I felt like I was a small child in school, being preached at, and talked down to.

At the time I found myself quite irritated, muttering and griping to myself. I didn't then know how to take it lightly. But in retrospect, cultivating Oma, I began to learn the principle of benign neglect! I came to just smile and head off to Graz as it suited me, not triggering to her unsolicited advice.

Back to the weeds: Oma sometimes treated her garden with benign neglect. Hers was not an immaculate garden, edges trimmed, with no clover or crab grass in the yard. The trees were not perfectly pruned, and weeds flourished in the herb garden. But the casual order and the sporadic weeds did not detract from the succulent sweetness of the peas freshly picked for the modest rice dish she was preparing for dinner. They didn't affect the tart splash of the juicy currants that exploded in your mouth, from which she made scrumptious preserves and tortes for afternoon coffee or dessert. Weeds were simply part of the garden.

The combination of cultivation and intention, together with acceptance and benign neglect, bore wonderful fruit and bestowed many gifts: crimson hollyhocks; delicate, lacy columbine; sweet, tiny forget-me-nots; cheerful, hardy sunflowers. A full range of nutritious fruits, veggies and herbs, balanced and life enhancing.

Oma didn't always live what she claimed to believe, yet she modeled for me in a way that made a lasting impression—to cultivate the beautiful and useful, savor the honey and honeysuckle along the way, and not to pay unnecessary attention to the weeds or irritations, only deal with them if they're choking other growing things.

We're always planting seeds, whether we are aware of it or not. We never know when we may have planted a seed that will bear fruit some time, some place. It's also probable, sometimes sooner, sometimes later, that we reap what we sow. Life as a garden is alive, and can enchant, instruct, and nourish ourselves and others.

Related reading:
Edwards, Betty ((1989). *Drawing on the Right Side of the Brain: A course in enhancing creativity and artistic confidence.* NY: G. P. Putnam's Sons
Haidt, Jonathan (2006). *The Happiness Hypothesis: Finding modern truth in ancient wisdom.* NY: Basic Books
Kingsolver, Barbara (2007). *Animal Vegetable, Miracle: A year of food life.* NY: HarperCollins
Sinetar, Marsha (1986). *Ordinary People As Monks and Mystics: Lifestyles for self-discovery.* Mahwah, NJ: Paulist Press

Reflections: *How does your garden grow? What sorts of seeds do you believe you are planting? If the fruit they bear are not exactly what you intended, what seeds would you like to plant and how could you nurture them? What are some 'weeds' in your garden and how do you relate to them? What are some aspects of your 'garden' that you particularly treasure and why?*

"Ain't no use hurryin' if you're on the wrong road." Satchel Paige

"The real voyage of discovery consists of not in seeking new landscapes but in having new eyes." Marcel Proust

∞✂∞

What a Trip!

I have made some extended cycling trips to destinations as far afield as Moose Jaw, Saskatchewan and Lafayette, Michigan. Often the toughest challenges of a journey occur when the going gets rough. When, on a bike or road trip, for example, there are flat-tires, poor signage, lousy shoulders, or pot-holed roads in jagged disrepair. Adding to the actual difficulty of the road's roughness, is that during such moments, the hard times take over; they inundate our minds and hearts, and become all we are capable of experiencing or remembering. As though we're in one massive, deep, and engulfing pothole. Enduring and surviving such times have led me to muse on the similarities between such a journey and life itself.

Rough seems forever, but it isn't. When I get out of bed, groggy for having gone to bed late the night before and having slept poorly, the day ahead seems very like a rough road. I stub my toe against the bed, drop my glasses and almost step on them as I brood over some impending decision. I feel overwhelmed, bummed out, frustrated. At that moment, I only manage to focus on the hard places right in front of me.

When we're experiencing the journey as a 'rough road,' we can, at least I do, blow all the rules about relationships and positive communication we've ever learned. We respond defensively, our timing is miserable, we don't listen or take the other person into account. It can feel more than rough. It can feel like quicksand. We're sinking down and will be swallowed up by the muck. (Sometimes it even feels as though that would be the preferred outcome.)

Yet inevitably, on a cycling trip, as in our lives, things will change. We never know what's around the next bend, but we can be sure, that sooner or later, things will be different. What a lesson. If only I could remember this lesson in the middle of the rough stretches.

On a particular trip in Manitoba, after a grueling climb, pedaling hard, feeling grouchy and tired (why did I get myself into this anyway?), we crested the hill and I took in a rainbow of wildflowers by the roadside, lush sprouting prairie fields, a grand panorama of cobalt sky, billows of white clouds. All this had been close at hand yet completely obscured from my view as I was huffing up the hill, swerving to miss the potholes, fearing the possibility of rain. What change. And virtually inconceivable from within the rough and struggle mode.

Being present to what is here now is transformative. One spring day I set out into the nearby park. As I began to jog, I was ruminating about an upcoming board meeting, how my view would be received, whether I'd done enough prep…embroiled in the past, burdened by the future.

But then, as I jogged along, something happened. I shifted gears. One could call it grace, willingness to be touched, to notice what is. I allowed and invited my eyes and soul to open. I became able to take in the shiny emerald of the new growth on the Douglas firs; the crimson, tangerine and ivory splendor of the rhododendron. My nose got a whiff of the clingy sweet smell of skunk cabbage, with its energetic, golden blossoms and luxurious leaves, and my ears admitted the softly murmuring stream. Senses throbbing, I was vital and grateful to be alive. Just then, at that moment, by myself in the woods.

Becoming: Journeying toward Authenticity

Simply cutting fruit for the morning fruit salad, can be a trip in itself. Almost like being on acid. When I am present, here and now. Usually I cut the fruit while thinking about the day to come, the e-mail that just came in, the weather. I'm traveling along, but paying no mind. But one different day stands out in my mind. I was there, in the kitchen, present with mind and body. I cut the fruit; slurped the mango juice; crunched the crisp Gala apple, striated red and yellow; felt the slip of the sharp knife splitting the grapefruit skin and its pungent oils as they sprayed my hand… If someone could see hearts, they would have perceived that mine was way bigger than my chest, radiating out into the kitchen, golden, glowing. I actually felt as though I didn't know myself in that moment, so different was that experience from my usual rut.

Is this brilliance and aliveness always available? Yes.

Am I always receptive? No. But I'm learning, in fits and starts, to pay attention.

Acceptance leads to trust; trust makes acceptance easier. It's a given that we do not know, or control, what's around the next bend. But the metaphor of life-as-a-journey also invites me to look at my attitude toward the not-knowing. Yes, things will change. But what about when we don't know how, or when, or whether what's to come will be smoother or rougher than what's here now. How do we hold the non-knowing itself?

Accepting not-knowing has been particularly tough for me. I like maps and plans, clarity and certainty. I like knowing where I'm going. When I'm taking pleasure in a smooth stretch, the journey metaphor helps me to remember that this too will change. But acceptance ain't automatic. Just when I think I've got the ticket and know the road, have the right gear, things are sure to change. Bummer.

How can I stay open to the unknown, to the mystery, to the unfolding? It seems simple, but it's not easy. I have found that when I am able to accept and rest in the not-knowing, a kind of basic trust can arise. Trust in the bigger mystery. After all, there can always, and surely often will, be a flat tire, or a sudden thunderstorm. A carefully thought out plan for getting from here to there may have to be completely revised. On the spot.

Living this awareness day to day, being with the impermanence, the changing, the flowing, is a life path. But even on the longest journey, I just need to put one foot in front of the other, take it one day at a time, one moment at a time, one flat tire or field of wildflowers, at a time.

The journey is the destination. Cycling off the ferry in Swartz Bay, bound for Victoria, to see our grandchildren, we were peddling up hill in the wake of exhaust fumes from the disembarking cars. Some fellow cyclists were grumpy and complaining. Yes, I knew we would ultimately be on the agreeable cycle path that runs all the way in from the ferry terminal to the core of downtown Victoria, but right now we were here, peddling uphill in exhaust fumes. I had a welling up of delight in that moment of insight: accepting the reality that the journey is the destination made all the difference. How I respond, in this moment, to what is here now, becomes my life. This is the journey; this is the destination.

What we resist persists. On my first significant cycle trip, over 2500 km from Vancouver to Eugene, Oregon and back, we had moderate or significant head winds most of the way. Every morning I would anxiously try to read the wind on the swaying of trees, flags, or whatever I could see moving. It was a nice relief if not much was moving, but frequently there was a noticeable wind. Figuring out the direction of the wind was usually disappointing. Many days, it turned out to be head wind. Again. This went on until well into our return trip.

One day I realized how much I'd been fighting it, struggling, wanting it to be different, and how much it was affecting me. I was carrying my resistance as an extra burden, which I really didn't need in addition to the camping stove, tent, sleeping bag, food, clothes, binoculars and camera I was already packing in my panniers.

That insight opened the way for a profoundly simple, yet

sweetly mysterious shift to occur. I stopped fighting and resenting the wind.

The day transformed. I slowed down inside, even when I was peddling hard, sensed my body, took in each breath deeply. Even though the wind was blowing in our faces, as it had many other days, somehow the colors got brighter, the people were friendlier, the hills less challenging. The food tasted better. I felt relief and pleasure, and relished the accomplishment of the many kilometers of the day's peddling in a way I had until then been unable to do. I had been carrying my additional attitudinal burden: Resistance to what is. On the road, and at any moment in life, my attitude affects the quality of the experience.

You won't believe what happened the day after I stopped resisting the wind. We had the strongest tail wind of the entire journey. The wind veritably carried us along, up a huge hill along the Hood Canal, pushing us forward, smiling in a kindly, blustery way on us wayfarers, and I smiled back. I felt like I had discovered a secret map, a way of exploring the territory that transformed even potholes, rough shoulders and headwinds from enemies to be dreaded or fought into simply other parts of the journey, to be wondered at, lived with, seen and absorbed.

I still like wide shoulders, smooth roads and tail winds, as probably you do too, if you cycle, or walk, or run, or drive. *And* (on better days!) I can also see the journey, including whatever I come across along the way, *as* the destination. And life as the journey.

Related reading:
De Botton, Alain (2002). *The Art of Travel*. NY: Vintage Books,
Random House
Elkins, James (2000). *How to Use Your Eyes*. NY: Routledge
Gilbert, Elizabeth (2007).). *Eat, Pray, Love: One woman's search for
everything across Italy, India and Indonesia*. NY: Penguin Books
Linnae, Ann ((1999). *Deep Water Passage: A spiritual journey at midlife*.
Boston: Simon & Schuster
Oliver, Mary (2004). *Long Life*. Cambridge, MA: Da Capo Press

Reflections: *Consider your life as a journey. What have been some of the
destinations? How do you experience the journey at times when there is a clear
destination and at times when it seems like you are lost? What has been your
attitude toward real or metaphorical potholes and headwinds? In what ways do
you resist your life's journey? What's the journey like when you don't resist?*

"Could a greater miracle take place than for us to look through each other's eyes for an instant." Henry Thoreau

"The skies, but not their souls, change for those who move across the sea." Horace

〜〜〜

People and Places

Related reading:
Bachelard, Gaston (1994). *The Poetics of Space: The classic look at how we experience intimate places.* Boston: Beacon Press
Eisler, Riane (1995). *The Chalice and the Blade: Our history, our future.* NY: HarperCollins
Leopold, Aldo (1948). *The Sand County Almanac.* Oxford: Oxford University Press
Pransky, George (2001). *The Relationship Handbook: A simple guide to more satisfying relationships.* Pransky and Associates
Thoreau, Henry (2004). *Walden.* Princeton: Princeton University Press

"There are two ways to live your life—one as though nothing is a miracle, the other is as though everything is a miracle." Albert Einstein

"Let us try to recognize the precious nature of each day." The 14th Dalai Lama

◦◦◦

Treasure Trove

Having grown up in a virtual desert, then lived some 20 years on the damp, dark and icy northern edge of the Alps, and now having spent two decades north of the 48th parallel, my occasional visits to the tropics stand out—like flashes of light or gleaming jewels.

Shall I tell you about the antediluvian frigate birds, circling lazy and casual in the cobalt sky as the sun dropped like a rock into the azure sea…. Or the cloud of great brown pelicans, in a bay off Malaque, hovering overhead, which, when spotting a school of fish near by, came plummeting into the water within a yard of where I was standing; or the scuba dive I took with a wizened biologist specializing in miniature, multi-colored nudibranchs; or the wild, seemingly interminable ride across the South China Sea in an outrigger, (luggage almost dangling over the side, feet too), where the engine died and the dolphin and flying fish accompanied us; or the manta rays at night, silently swooping, dark, slow, quick, gleaming, glinting; or the giant sea turtles that loomed out of the grey-green turgidity into sight, seemingly to greet me, then lazing on by; or swimming through the breathtaking rainbow splashes of tropical fish: the angels, damsels, neons, unicorns, parrots, wrasses… and how they leave multi-colored imprints in my psyche that still lift my heart on grey days; or the unexpected discovery of the octopus, the wall of sun stars; oh, maybe the heart-stopping snorkel where I came face to teeth with a crocodile only 4 feet away…

I think I'll tell you about the scuba dive where I met, most unexpectedly, the pod of lumbering, secretive, gargantuan parrot fish.

I was volunteering with a conservation organization to map coral reefs so that local governments and non-profits working together could plan wise use and take steps to halt the ongoing and wanton destruction. It was Sunday, and a day off from our weekday work of diving transects and recording the fish and coral we observed. On this day we were allowed to take a recreational dive. No need to swim straight lines, carrying waterproof pad and pencil to record every thing that moved, and much of what didn't. We could just dive where and how we wished, roaming slo-mo in the warm, limpid underworld, following our fancy. Of course you always dove with an assigned buddy. As it happened I was assigned Stu, a lug of the bunch. Stu was just out of high school, full of himself, quick with jokes that weren't very funny, even to his contemporaries, a wanna-be dude… In short, just my kinda guy. (Not!)

Well, if I felt I had been mis-paired, you can imagine what Stu felt. With all those other guys he'd like to have impressed and some good looking chicks to choose from, he had to get stuck with the granny of the group, whom, up to that point, he may well not even have noticed. Being ignored or overlooked can have its advantages. As I age I find I have the opportunity to enjoy these positives more and more often! And that day I (and Stu) wished I had been overlooked by the capo making the dive assignments that day. But no, Stu and I were to be dive partners.

We looked at each other a bit wryly, and he, uncharacteristically graciously, muttered something like 'I didn't do it.' And we set off, donning the piles of gear, checking our gauges, air, regulators. As we descended into the mild deep blue, giving each other the thumb-first finger circle of OK, it seemed like it was going to be a routine outing. I almost wished it were over, and I could lounge on the beach, or rock in the hammock reading the book I had on the go, rather than attending to the details of the dive. But when you've paid to volunteer, it seems important to get in all the diving possible, take every opportunity to submerge.

I don't mean to sound blasé. It's kind of like getting up each morning. I can have the attitude 'Oh, another day (dive.) Ho, hum.' Or I can open my eyes and ears, breathe deeply, feel the air enter my body through the miraculous apparatus of lungs (a demand valve which marvelously supplies me with breathing gas at ambient pressure). I can be in touch with my environment, air or water, with fresh eyes, open to see the newness of each moment. Sometimes I need to remind myself that there's a choice involved, each moment, for stale or fresh. So on that day with Stu, I resisted the tendency to wish the dive over and began to pay close attention.

As we dove steadily deeper, we equalized our air pressure, and each clearing of my ears was a signal that I was entering further into other creatures' territory, into their world, where, compared to them, I was definitely different and obviously awkward. But I enjoy the adapting as well, slowing down, noticing how the colors fade with each passing foot, how the populations of fish and coral shift through the descent.

There was an array of fish that day, the bright small ones, darting, flashing orange, cadmium, neon blue, red and black in and among the undulating soft corals, the fans, the sea pens. Then there were some larger, nautically perambulating groupers, and the occasional porcupine or box fish. Stu and I checked in with each other. 'Dive going OK?' Circle thumb and forefinger signaling 'Yes. Carry on.'

I swam closer to the walls of coral and looked close-up at the array of shapes, the intricacy of the systems for feeding, the delicate polyps and the waving antennae. I was relieved just to be able to let their forms and colors, the feeling of intrigue at the variety, simply soak into my senses without having to recall the exact names and write them all down.

Diving in a tropical coral reef feels like I have been dropped into a living treasure trove: that I am immersed in a secret world, with riches so unbelievable, so fantastic, that I can hardly remember the full effect of the magic when I return to land and am obliged to set about sweeping the sand so the biting flies can't lay their eggs to plague us the next day, or shoveling the smelly accumulation in the composting toilet that serves our camp. When I'm down there with the fish and coral, all regular work, concepts of land time and normal life are suspended. I am allowed to float with and through the jewels, melting and mingling. Taking it in, flowing with.

And then I lifted my gaze up, looked out to sea, many meters away, where the water was not quite so clear as it is close up. I squinted. What was that? What were those? I nudged Stu and he looked too. A bit dim, shadowy at first, some shapes began to emerge. Large. Very large, and getting even larger as they swam closer. Neither of us had ever seen them, but we knew at once that we had been gifted an encounter with a group of giant bumphead parrot fish. There were about six of them, each about four feet long and pretty thick around the middle, coming toward us. Not common. Usually fish swim away but the seemingly gentle colossuses moseyed ever closer. We froze on the spot, holding as still as we could, and I felt my heart start to pound.

Then just as casually and as silently as they had come, the parrot fish moved on, and Stu and I were left, approaching the end of our dive, staggered. We signaled each other to ascend, to let this be our denouement. As we drifted up, slowly to let our ears and air pressure adjust in our systems, we kept looking at each other and grinning through our goggles, bubbles oozing out the edges. Stu and I had a special connection now, the inopportune pairing having turned us into providential partners. We had trouble containing ourselves as we unpacked, undressed, stowed our gear and returned to camp where we then told of our good fortune. We were bubbling over with our felicitous experience.

It had been with reluctance and reticence that I embarked on the dive that day, and yet the day had ended with open hearted gratitude and a spreading sense of companionship that included Stu but wasn't restricted to him, it spread out and on. I'd made my first choice on the way down: not to consider it just another dive, not wishing I'd been somewhere else, with someone else, but to bring my fullest to being there, then. How many days do I miss this opportunity and just glaze over, dull down, slog through? More than I'd like to admit. Yes, I make it though those days too, but at what loss? Many spiritual teachers speak of the way we waste our time, how we have a precious opportunity being alive, being human. How easy it is to forget these exhortations and squander or slop through our days, our time.

The bumpback parrot fish stand out like a freeze frame in my memory, and the exuberance in being alive; the warmth and gratitude I felt after that dive do as well.

But does it *have* to be something extraordinary that jolts me into my fullest? Actually I know it doesn't. At times when I have just been with myself, sensing deeply, breathing and being, I have wound up feeling just as 'high,' touched by life. And my daily doings on those occasions have been equally transformed, taking on a quality of preciousness, a glow and liveliness that contrasts radically with the daily hum-drum days when I'm not really there, not really in my body or paying attention. But does it have to be parrot fish? Couldn't I just as well allow my heart to be opened by the smile on my daughter's face, or a butterfly in the dahlias, or the tang of orange juice on my tongue?

The answer is yes.

Related reading:

Adyashanti (2000). *The Impact of Awakening*. Los Gatos, CA: Open Gate Publishing

Elkins, James (2000). *How to Use Your Eyes*. NY: Routledge

Ram Dass (1978). *Be Here Now*. Kingsport, TN: Hanuman Foundation

Thich Nhat Hanh (1996). *Breathe! You Are Alive*. Berkeley: Parallax Press

Reflections: *What are some life experiences that you hold as treasures? Why do you consider them treasures? When in your life is it particularly tempting to go numb, to check out? What is one example? Think or write about that experience as if you had been fully present and describe how this experience might have affected you?*

"There are no seven wonders of the world in the eyes of a child. There are seven million." Walt Streightiff

"Every child you encounter is a divine appointment." Wess Stafford

Children

All the other mothers in the neighborhood were secretly, or not even so secretly, thrilled when school started again in the fall, and their little darlings were finally out of the house again for much of the day—relieved and grateful to have their lives back again. My mom shared this with me when I was a young mother myself. Then she added that it wasn't that way for her at all. She was always sad when the school bells rang. She treasured the long summer days where her children were home. It meant precious time together playing puzzles and games, having quiet time in the afternoon, reading and discussing, swimming and hitting tennis balls.

There was something else in her tone that rang through and rang true. In many ways, my mother truly valued children. I appreciate this about her, and I took her as a model in this. "Jill," she said, "never to talk down to your children. Treat them like real people."

At the time I was startled. Not because I had ever experienced her talking down. I have not a single recollection of condescension, being shushed, or required to defer to adults. At family dinners our views as children, and adolescents, were always welcomed. Having that conversation with my mother refreshed and sharpened my appreciation and respect for her that our challenging mother-daughter interactions had at times blurred or tainted. She was aware of the presents that children are and offer. Remembering how she valued her children sets off sparks for me, like a turning, gleaming kaleidoscope.

As I write this, my husband Mike and I have ten grandchildren between us, and we have had the privilege of spending sufficient time with many of them from early on in their lives to follow their unfolding, to treasure and track their uniqueness as they develop. Being a grandparent is so blessedly different from the semi-unconscious way I parented, bouncing from apple crisp to raging crises, from dirty laundry to doctor's appointments. To savor unfettered by quotidian responsibility the inestimable gift of human birth and new life, the delicate, wispy, caress and the bouquet of a baby's fragrance as it nuzzles, puppy-like, into the space between your neck and shoulder, and rests there completely content, trusting, at ease—what bliss. But I wax grandparenty.

I treasure specific, vivid views into life's profusion that grandchildren have opened in my life. They, and we, are plasma, forming, morphing, adapting, choosing what helps us survive and thrive. It's like being inside a time-warp laboratory, taking part in how children embody essence, true nature and at the same time are personalities becoming. Electrifying and illuminating.

I recall and relive regularly how Anika, about four at the time, burst into our front hall after we'd all been for an outing along the seawall, flinging her arms in an ebullient vee in the air, saying, "Who wants to play with the amazing me?" What confidence and clarity! How in touch she was with essential joy and aliveness. When I feel dank inside, out of touch with myself, when I am focused on the jaggedness rather than the rainbow of life's kaleidoscope, I sometimes remember, and it is a gift when I do, to feel Anika's exuberance, there in all of us, accessible if we but tap in.

Each child has sparked and lit up my life in abundant ways, and this list must not be taken to limit or define any child. It is, however, rewarding to recall the uniqueness of each one, and articulate some explicit ways each one has opened me to essential qualities, fresh, flowing out of their being into our field together, enriching me and others.

I relearn awe and wonder, frequently buried beneath my daily humdrum. As I see Gabriella, at one and a half, lean into the aquarium glass to watch, with no knowledge of evolutionary theories, nomenclature, or taxonomy, the darting neons or golden wrasses, pointing and smiling at the boxy, bizarre porcupine fish, I tap in to reverence for the glorious nameless, and the breathtaking variety about us. I am humbled when I realize the ignorant numbness with which I often take it all for granted, and sense my gratitude for being able to spend time with the likes of her.

When Lilly came into the world, among the youngest of the assembly, perfection, innocence, and sweetness climbed right out of the pictures of her and into my heart. Because she lives far away we do video chats to stay in touch. Ah, the wonders of technology. What charm to share Lilly's impish giggle as she touches our images on the computer screen and sees us laugh and play tickled across the miles, yet right there in her living room. Her capacity to be both light and concerned (for example, when we sing her a silly ditty about mice cavorting and then losing their rear appendages to a fearsome carving knife), connected yet puzzled, reminds me that we can hold contradictory experiences simultaneously and be open to them both.

When Maceo was about three I had a chance to be with him in the woods; we encountered some clearings, but also much tangle and underbrush. I watched him plunge ahead, picking himself up literally countless times, sometimes from significant face plants, intrepid, unfazed, with determination and fierceness. At times I need, and am grateful to have, Maceo as a model in my life. Courage, will, strength.

From about three months to her now almost four years, I have basked in the glow that emanates from Marlena's face, her unselfconscious, spontaneous beam, her essential joy in being alive. A perennial wonder is how the internal radiance and contentment can be coupled with the outgoing joie de vivre that takes her into a stranger's yard, fearless, curious, expansive. The grace that Marlena fashioned on a summer afternoon, "Out in the garden, under an umbrella, eating cheese and raisins," is my life haiku for pleasure in what is, and gratitude that we may partake of it.

As an infant, Nick may have been the smilingest child I've ever seen. It took nothing more than a peek over his bassinet or carrier for him to literally explode into a full bodied grin, often with gurgling sound effects. Day or night. With family or strangers. Basic trust. Watching Nick at about one (his mom a gentle, holding presence in the background), as he touches wind chimes and listens to their mellow harmonies, I share in his wonder, soft surprise, and enchantment. As he kicks a soccer ball at three I am taken over by his capacity, concentration, and enjoyment.

Recalling Noah, as an infant, submitting to the required 'car seat challenge,' sitting calmly while the adults check whether he is strong enough to ride in a car and go home, I contact resilience, the inherent strength and capacity to take what comes along, unperturbed. Sitting together, having carved out special time together for a while on his sixth birthday, talking about how we can feel our chests expand to include the whole world, becoming the lion on an African savannah, and then just feeling ourselves, there, on the rock beside the lake, full, alive. We are personal, real, contactful, present.

A child teaches me to use my eyes and ears in new and vibrant ways. Walking with Oliver at two or three, slowing to his time, watching through his eyes, pausing with him to look at a leaf or a twig, I see these afresh, touch and feel the textures on my skin, let in the delicacy or the rough irregularity. I become open, permeable, fluid. Oliver reminds me how sharp in perception we can be, how we integrate in subtle ways. I see him quietly pondering what he sees, hears, and marvel how, days or weeks later, he will bring forth a full blown observation or insight.

Watching Orla color a picture, play the piano, demonstrate her Irish dancing, I share, self-remembering, in her energetic focus, attention, full presence. She is here. Now. Then she looks up, at ease with herself and her functioning. Orla reminds me that I can be absorbed, alert *and* in touch with spacious, inclusive expansiveness.

We have occasion to visit Rowen at home, travel with her, have her stay with us. In all those circumstances, equanimity is what comes to mind. She has a way of calming the environment and the people in it. Seeing her reach out her tiny, pale hand, with simplicity and warmth, to touch the passive, dark arm of her massive accidental neighbour on the subway system, the rumbling world beneath New York City, experiencing him melt into a full bodied smile, and then feeling my own melting, merging, and sharing the glow with others, is a touchstone for contact and softness in the midst of our clanging, jangling urban worlds.

As Henry Ward Beecher says, "children are the hands by which we take hold of heaven;" they are our guides and teachers; not just simply miracles, but constant reminders of the precious uniqueness of us all; they touch our deepest being, our true nature, remind us of our unlimited potential and invite us to realize our full capacities. We have a responsibility to mirror their aliveness, give them every opportunity to just be, and to be fully themselves. Thus doing, we ourselves are truly living as well.

Related Reading:

Almaas, A. H. (2008). *The Unfolding Now: Realizing your true nature through the practice of presence.* Boston: Shambhala

Dillard, Annie (1987). *An American Childhood.* NY: Harper & Row

Fulghum, Robert (2003). *All I Really Need to Know I Learned in Kindergarten.* NY: Random House

Mahler, Margaret (1975). *The Psychological Birth of the Human Infant: Symbiosis and individuation.* NY: Basic Books

Milne, A, A, (1994). *The Complete Tales of Winnie-the-Pooh.* NY: Dutton Children's Books

Reflections: *What role do children play in your life and how do you relate to them? What have you learned by being in their presence? If you have children and grandchildren, what have you learned as a parent that you might do differently as a grandparent? If you have grandchildren, what can you do, how can you be, to encourage them to shine, to be themselves? How might your story be different if someone had done that for you as a child?*

Granddaughter Casey (4), on hearing that her great-grandma Jane (86) was her mother's grandmother: "She can't be a mother—she's too old and she can't take care of anyone."

"Perhaps the greatest social service that can be rendered by anybody to the country and to mankind is to bring up a family." George Bernard Shaw

ͻͼͽ

What's a Mother?

The sun lit the little maple table as I sat down that spring morning to breakfast. It splashed light on the new green of the cactus, making it as shiny and lush as the fruit on the cereal I was having. My son, Martin, a young adult by then, was here for a few days to help me settle in after a big move to Vancouver, and in a cheerful mood. The warmth and relaxation of the companionship and good company were unspoken but palpable, as was a sense of accomplishment and excitement of new beginnings. Grateful for what I perceived as our shifting roles as parent and child, I commented, "I am so glad I don't have to be your mother anymore."

Martin looked at me, puzzled. "But I want you to be my mother. Don't say that!"

"Well, I've been in that role for years and I'm actually quite treasuring the way it's changing." He was silent for a few moments, seemingly perplexed and a bit apprehensive. I wondered why Martin would not be glad at this shift and maturing of our relationship. It was fresh to me, a relief, an unexpected gift. But he continued to be silent, and I didn't know what to say either. I began to get concerned at his silence and distance.

Fortunately, and before too much longer, it dawned on me

Becoming: Journeying toward Authenticity

to check out what we each meant when we used the word 'mother.' I started off. "My mom had many positive qualities and there is no doubt in my mind that she loved me and my brother very much. But one of the main messages I got from her, and kept getting even as I became an adult, was that I was usually not doing something 'right.' She was often critical of one thing or another. Even when I had long since grown up, I still often felt that I was disappointing her. It was the pits."

"Yikes," Martin said, "that sounds awful."

"It *was* pretty hard and we never entirely got past it. Neither of us knew how to resolve it or clear things up. I felt hurt, and didn't know how to tell her, and I think she felt betrayed by the choices I had made. I think she had hoped and expected that I would live a life much like hers. When I married a European and wound up living abroad on a shoestring, she was disappointed. More than that, I believe she felt that I was rejecting her and her values. I remember her saying one day, 'Jill, you don't want anything we have, do you.' It wasn't a question. It was a statement. There was bitterness and pain in her voice. I took her statement to be a judgment of my values, my choices, my lifestyle."

As I was talking to Martin I remembered an incident. Years ago, when my mom heard that I was going to continue my education in Europe, she burst out in tears, abruptly left the room and never mentioned it again. Dad had later tried to explain to me how disappointed she was, how hurt and rejected she felt. I needed encouragement and support at the time, and instead, I felt pushed away. I was self-focused and didn't have the maturity or empathy to respond to her disappointment with curiosity, let alone compassion. Had I been able to respond differently, the dynamic might have shifted. Perhaps we could have had a conversation that would have opened some doors to each other's worlds. As it was, doors were slammed shut with a deafening echo, creating a painful barrier between us.

I turned to Martin, still sitting there at the breakfast table, and continued, "The way she talked to me, or sometimes *didn't* talk to me, felt like blame and critique. As if I was living *my* life to hurt *her*! I have worried about you and Lisl at times, but I haven't wanted you to feel criticized like that. And sometimes being a mom feels almost like a double bind. On the one hand, I am not responsible for your life and I don't want to be critical of your choices. At the same time, I *do* believe that as your mother I have an obligation to see that you get a reasonable education, have some options in life, that you don't fall in holes too deep to get out of, and learn a few manners so you can be comfortable when you are having tea with the queen!"

Again I drifted back several years to my early mothering struggles, to a long ago sleepless night. Awake with a child of two at the foot of our bed, I wondered, planned, weighed… What kind of education could I offer my children? How can we have a bi-lingual home? How do I choose wisely and 'get it right'?

I came back again to Martin and offered "As your mom, I often felt a push-pull, worry versus trust. And now, at last, it feels like I'm done with that, that we can be friends, enjoy adventures together, and just hang out. And I'm relishing that. It feels to me like a new beginning, full of potential, unknown, open-ended—just like this new apartment and my new life here in Vancouver." This discussion was clarifying my understanding of some of what being a mother comprised for me. And what a mix of qualities it was!

Martin smiled, leaned back in his chair, got up and gave me a hug. "Well, for me a mother is someone who loves you in and out, up and down. Kinda like 'home is where, when you go there, they take you in, no matter what,'" he said. "A mom'll help out when you're in trouble and maybe even do your laundry sometimes. You are mine, and I'm glad. Not perfect, of course, not always what I wanted," he grinned. "I remember when you washed my mouth out with soap! You didn't *have* to do that! What I'd said was bad, but not *that* bad!"

The picture continued to get clearer: Our both having heard the words "I'm so glad I don't have to be your mother anymore" was a common experience. But what these words meant to each of us was completely different. For me, the word 'mother' called up for me a picture of someone responsible, always trying to figure out what was best for her children...

As much as I treasured being a mom, my associations with the word 'mother' were, at least in part, sufficiently dark and dank that I wanted to redefine or drop them. High expectations, and the lurking anxiety of not doing right by my children felt heavy and burdensome to me. I hadn't really explored my fears and anxieties as a mom, and I couldn't even define them precisely. But they were present in the wings, murky yet heightened by all the media articles and images that made it sound possible, even quite easy, to be a perfect mother—to be there for your children, and to make sensible choices between encouraging kids' freedom and independence, and at the same time guiding them smoothly through the many rocks and hard places of growing up. I was more than ready to be freed from those expectations and tough choices!

Martin's words cleared the air. Despite the fact that I had not always been there for him, had not always listened to him openly, and despite the fact that I had sometimes been preoccupied with my own struggles, Martin's understanding of motherhood was imbued with warmth and acceptance. It relieved and surprised me.

I asked him to tell me more. "Oh, I remember an example," Martin said. "My best buddy Marcus. Remember? We were always building things—rockets, skateboards...we made so many things together as kids. Marcus's mom would always say things like 'That's nice, but why don't you try this? If you added this or that, it would be even better.' But when we showed *you* our projects, you'd just say 'Wow. That's cool! Nice job.' I loved that about you."

I could hardly believe it! Had I really been that accepting?

The morning was wearing on, and as I wanted to go to a furniture store in hopes of finding the perfect sofa bed, we ended the conversation there. As we drove off, I had a sunny feeling in my chest. I smiled and relished the connection we had just had, the sharing of lives and meanings. And all of it the result of such a simply exploring what mother meant to each of us.

I said to Martin, " So with a little luck we can be the kind of grown up friends I'd like us to be, and I can also, continue to be the kind of mom you think you've had up to now! Not sure about the laundry though. How about we share that!"

This lightness was not quite in proportion to the significance of a conversation that I felt had gently but profoundly altered our worlds and changed the way we understood our roles individually and together. The experience of our sharing and the memory of the images and anecdotes has lingered on to this day.

Driving home that day after shopping for furniture, we got caught in rush hour traffic. The sun was setting over the city, and there was a pink afterglow that felt like the lingering warmth in the skin after a sunny afternoon on the beach. I reached over to touch Martin's hand.

Related reading:

Bombeck, Irma (2005). *When God Created Mothers.* Kansas City: Andrews McMeel Publishing

Richardson, Ronald (1995). *Family Ties That Bind: A self-help guide to change through family of origin therapy.* North Vancouver, BC: International Self-Counsel Press

Schwartz, Richard (1997). *Internal Family Systems Therapy.* NY: The Guilford Press

Reflections: *What does the word mother mean to you? What do you think it meant to your mother? To your children, if you have any? If you were to have a real or imaginary conversation with your mother about what mothering meant, what would you like to say? Perhaps you can do an exercise with two chairs. When you sit in one, speak for yourself, and in the other, speak as you think your mother might speak. On completion of the exercise, what new information emerged, if any?*

"Love is a choice you make moment to moment." Barbara de Angelis

"Have no fear of perfection—you'll never reach it." Salvador Dali

◌◌◌

Cybil's Advice

The train's wheels were clicking us along on our way to Ravenna, Italy. The clarified Umbrian light illuminated a wizened, grey-haired grandmother (who was a close family friend), and me (a young mother of two, early in a challenging first marriage). We were traveling together on a day trip, away from our partners, children and tour groups. Cybil leaned over close to me that day and began to speak softly, almost whispering. As she bent toward me, she paused, and then said, "Jill, don't ever withhold sex as a punishment." Taken aback and abashed, I didn't press for more information at the time, but these words stayed with me and occasionally guided my actions.

Cybil's marriage was long and loyal even though she was in a constant sparring match with her husband, Joel. Both witty and erudite, they both wanted to be right, and verbal jousting was their daily fare. The atmosphere at their house, although punctuated by hits of laughter, was often not relaxing or comfortable to be around.

While it's often easy for us to see other people's shortcomings in communicating with each other, it's a different matter to recognize and deal effectively with communication challenges in one's own life. At first glance, miscommunication and crunchy verbal interactions seem to occur much like wind storms and rainy weather. Misunderstandings seem just to happen now and then, arising either as a result of intentional jousting, or inadvertently because of assumptions, old patterns, the prevalent human tendency to take things personally... These patterns, challenges and tangles exist in same sex as well as heterosexual relationships.

I think of several painful encounters between my partner and me where something I said, or a hand gesture I made, was taken to be hurtful or dismissive. 'Oh, it wasn't such a big deal, I didn't really mean it, don't be so sensitive,' I would think. Worse, I might even have said it aloud because my first impulse is often self-serving, and an effort to make myself look or feel good. Sometimes my partner got reactive in response. His behavior toward me became cold and distant. If he said anything at all, it might have been something like "That's the same pattern we were just talking about. You'll never learn. You really are just like your mother." And there we were again—both stuck in reactivity and old patterns.

At such times, not only is sexual intimacy far from my mind, I sometimes want to refuse any form of communication or closeness as a way of demonstrating just how hurt and angry I feel. I have even felt the inclination to 'punish' the other by declining. And I can imagine this is exactly what Cybil might have meant. Don't bring sexuality into the fray when it's other issues that are surfacing. And in this context, it's good advice indeed.

Along the journey, doing the dance, I've learned ways to check in with myself, clear with the other, address glitches and breakdowns with some curiosity and lightness. But this was not always so, and Cybil's words, "Don't withhold sex as a punishment," were help along the way. When my partner's sexual interest emerges when I'm in the middle of something—doing dishes, reading, or giving close attention to a project—I find I am often strongly disinclined to be sexual. Or there might arise a tangle of feelings: misunderstanding, hurt... On better days, I intuitively connected with Cybil's wisdom: that it was not only inappropriate, it would very likely make things worse. I was able to grasp that withdrawing sexually, while easy and even comforting, was not smart, would serve neither me nor us.

On the other hand, for men and women, men and men, women and women, to get along, it's healthy and smart to move toward each other, to understand each other's modus operandi, even to try out the different modes. So there were times when I moved toward my partner, didn't 'withhold sex' even when I didn't particularly feel like engaging sexually.

When I made this choice, the results were sometimes unexpectedly satisfying: I sometimes felt close after all. It also sometimes happened, and not uncommonly, that we had the kind of clarifying, connecting conversation for which I had been yearning. We both moved out of our patterns and toward each other. We were able to talk, not only about sexuality, different preferences, rhythms, fantasies, times and locations, but also about the very misunderstandings that had been hanging in the air.

While this may not always be the choice to make, at least I know there are times when going with my partner's desires, even when they are not mine in the moment, can lead to greater intimacy, and not just sexually.

Some of our rich and detailed conversations have been about lovemaking and sex itself—about the different ways we see it, feel it, live it, want it, love it. It took some courage to start these talks, but once we got going, we both found it exciting and transformative. I believe it is a partial result of some of these conversations that I was able to move from a very limited, localized climax, (like the ones I first experienced as a little girl, lying in bed, not knowing what was happening, but enjoying it a lot!), to a mature, rich, full-bodied orgasm or several. Without talking together about the different ways we experienced orgasm, and the build-up to it, what helped us get there (images, touch, fantasies, closeness), I would probably have remained bound by my familiar, limited

Becoming: Journeying toward Authenticity

experiences for the rest of my years.

The conversations also helped us bridge some of our differences. Knowing the intense way visual images play a role in my partner's sexuality and sense of intimacy has helped me to make changes in some of my actions in lovemaking. It helped me to understand my partner better. And my lover was intrigued to learn about the particular, individual ways I heighten my awareness, feel close, invite and encourage my libido, especially when it didn't happen to be raging at the moment! For me visuals are not as important as touch and softness, slowing down. But sometimes a quick pace can elicit fireworks as well. I never know ahead of time. We've been moving toward each other through, and linked by, our differences.

As I've aged, Cybil's words still ring true. Punishment has no place in a healthy, mature relationship, in sex or anywhere else. We may sometimes not be in an erotic or sensuous mood, but it's nice to know it's not about withholding sex. It might be that we're both just sleepy!

Keeping the lines of communication open has proven key for my partner and me. I have a hunch that the words Cybil whispered to me on the train to Ravenna might have come out of that awareness. As I've talked with my women friends, around campfires or over tea, under the stars, across the years, it seems generally true: as couples have stagnated and become stuck in familiar patterns, periods of shut down and diminished interest or capacity for sexuality have followed suit. This, in my opinion, almost inevitably occurs in long-term relationships. It's part of the flow, the peaks and valleys. And possibly also part of the learning.

Yet when partners recommit to the journey, began to dance again and look where they wanted to go, intimacy and good sex often return as part of the new landscape. Then the relationship and the sex can be as good as new.

Related reading:
Gray, John (1992). *Men Are from Mars, Women Are from Venus*. NY: HarperCollins
Lerner, Harriet (1989). *The Dance of Anger: A woman's guide to changing the patterns of intimate relationships.* NY: Harper & Row
Moore, Thomas (1994). *SoulMates: The mysteries of love.* NY: Harper Perennial
Tannen, Deborah (1990). *You Just Don't Understand: Women and men in conversation.* NY: Ballantine Books
Wilber, Ken (2000). *Sex, Ecology, Spirituality: The spirit of evolution.* Boston: Shambhala

Reflections: *How do you respond when you and your partner are out of sync? How can you stay true to yourself and sill connected and in relationship when is it challenging to do so? What are the costs when you're not attuned to yourself? How does the quality of communication with your intimate partner(s) affect your sex life?*

*"In America sex is an obsession, in other
parts of the world it is a fact."* Marlene Dietrich

*"The notion that each moment can be the completely fresh start of a
completely new future continues to thrill me and inspire me,
whenever I remember it."* Harvey Jackins

∾

Romantic and Sexual Intimacy

S exuality is so delicate, so precious, and so charged with layers
and levels of emotions, politics, power, love, fear, pleasure,
neediness… While there are a variety of relationships that
are asexual, it's incontrovertible that sexuality is an integral part of
humanity's long haul. And for most of us, an intimate relationship
includes sexuality, more or less, sooner or later.

Much research has been done on both male and female
sexual behavior, preferences, practices. The patterns and statistics
are intriguing, illuminating, contradictory, and provocative. As
I delved into the material I realized that what encourages and
heartens me is our uniqueness and our capacity to change and
experiment. I find it touching and challenging that each one
of us, regardless of studies, statistics or prevalent patterns, has the
opportunity to decide how we will act, what romantic inclinations
we will follow, or not. At any given moment afresh.

So what about those convoluted situations where conflict, or
even simply misunderstandings or differences with a partner, lead
one to feel emotionally distant and out of touch? How can we
respond when feeling angry, hurt *and* turned on all at the same
time? What about when I feel close, and my partner doesn't?
What takes priority when I experience conflicting thoughts and
emotions? What are the costs of overriding my thoughts, drives or

emotions? And how do these questions actually play out in the bedroom?

For some people, typically women, but not exclusively, and particularly in an ongoing relationship, an emotional connection feels like a prerequisite for an interest in making love. What to do when this connection is lacking, but the situation is getting warmer? For example, there have been those times in the middle of the night when my partner has moved close and been turned on, but I was not. Maybe I was sleepy. Perhaps I was still carrying some residue from a previous misunderstanding or interaction, but maybe it wasn't about communication this time at all.

Regardless of the reasons underlying how I was feeling in the moment, the relevant question then became whether I was willing to meet my partner sexually. At such times I may have recalled Cybil's heartfelt and surprisingly intimate advice, and put the question to myself, 'Withhold or not withhold?' That is a question, no doubt. But is it a relevant one, or not applicable? If relevant, how do I answer it?

There have been times when I decided, along, I suspect, with women over the centuries, millennia, to reciprocate my partner's sexual advances out of fear—fear of losing touch or losing love. This may seem, or actually be, sad and unhealthy, but this is no place for reproach or blame. Whenever this has happened, it was the best any of us could do at the time. I was afraid of being alone, and I didn't know how to be true to myself in relationship.

Viewing life as a dance, it seems that at that time in my life I just didn't know very many different steps—I didn't see many options. As I began to look where I wanted to go, I began to learn other dances, other rhythms, see other options. Now I can view this time in my life with curiosity and compassion and not fault myself for my fears and limitations.

What I find more revealing, though, are the times when I decided, in part with Cybil's words in mind, to engage, to lean toward love, not out of fear. Noticing that I didn't actually feel close, I chose, consciously, to come toward and not back or push away. Frequently I found that by doing this, the lack of closeness I experienced at first began to evolve, shifting, slowly at first, and I felt something delicate seeping into me, oozing into my pores, breathing into my body intimacy and responsiveness. It was interesting to me in retrospect that doing what I wasn't inclined to do, actually shifted my own experience, as well as the dynamics in my relationship.

Yet there are times when there might be something more in the wings. I certainly believe there are times when listening to the 'no,' or 'not now,' is important. Yet before acting on the 'no,' I find it useful to ask myself some questions. Am I being true to myself or maybe just ornery? Am I subtly (or not so subtly) withholding affection, and if so why? Resentment? Assumptions? Imbalance? Irritability? History? Am I inclined to rebuff rather than accommodate my partner? Why, and is this ever appropriate? How can I acknowledge my feelings, and yet not have them be the whole show, or the final and only arbiter, in a situation? Do I want just to decline sexual contact altogether, or might I want ask for something in return, or preceding the connection?

If we have the courage to get to know ourselves better, in part by asking the hard questions, either in the moment or afterward, either to ourselves in private or to share them out loud, who knows what will happen. We'll move toward authenticity, we'll discover nooks and crannies of ourselves that we probably didn't know existed. And we can share them in the moment, or just taste, savor and digest the morsels. And we might just be surprised what we find as we dare to be curious and honest…

If I so choose, I might behave in a completely different way tomorrow from anything I've ever done before. Each day a new dance. Each night… Who knows? This freshness is freedom, always available, ever possible.

Related reading:
Fromm, Erich (1956). *The Art of Loving.* NY: Harper & Row
Gottman, John (1994). *Why Marriages Succeed and Fail: And how you can make yours last.* NY: Simon & Schuster
Lerner, Harriet (1989). *The Dance of Intimacy: A woman's guide to courageous acts of change in key relationships.* NY: Harper & Row
Psaris, Jett and Marlena Lyons (2000). *Undefended Love.* Oakland, CA: New Harbinger Publications
Welwood, John (1996). *Love and Awakening: Discovering the sacred path of intimate relationship.* NY: HarperCollins

Reflections: *What has been the ebb and flow of your sexuality? What role does it play in your life and how do you feel about this? What would you still like to experience sexually? How important to is an emotional connection with a sexual partner to you? On what does it depend?*

"By seeing the beauty in every face, we lift others into their wisest self, and increase the chances of hearing a synchronistic message." James Redfield

"Strangers are exciting, their mystery never ends. But, there's nothing like looking at your own history in the faces of your friends." Ani Defranco

◈〜◈

The Face

Sometimes when I notice lines as they begin to appear on my face, I have a certain detachment. At other times I feel surprise, and occasionally a gripping sense of loss when I see new changes revealed in a glance, a comment, or a photograph. Years ago, for example, we were on a family ski vacation in Italy. It was a sunny day and I was in good spirits. As we were riding up the ski lift, my former husband reached over and touched my face, tracking the line a smile dimple made on my cheek and said, "There's the first one." He was observing that the line was now permanent, not disappearing after a smile like it used to do. I did not feel joyful at his observation.

Changes sometimes seem to come overnight. Visiting my parents in the midwest, I was brushing my teeth one morning and was struck by the texture of my skin. It was no longer smooth the way it had been the last time I looked. It suddenly seemed puckered, noticeably less firm and fine grained. That look in the mirror made a lasting impression.

This was all before I had heard about the Buddhist teaching of impermanence. Everything, without exception, is always in flux. But does it have to apply to my face? Yes, it does. Things were certainly changing and will continue to change. Yet we do have some choices.

Several decades ago I saw my face on a photograph and it was like peering into a looking glass of the future. We were in South Tyrol with the kids for an autumn celebration the Austro-Italians call Toerggelen. The Tyroleans know how to live it up. They distribute the new wine liberally. The fruits of the field are spread out in each farmhouse, and locals and tourists alike can taste of them and fill up. My family and I were out for a walk.

Unbeknownst to me, someone shot a picture of me as I was taking in the scenes, with nothing particular on my mind. On the photo, my mouth inscribed an upside-down happy face. There were deep downward lines of my mouth, a drawn forehead, an overall look of discontent. What made the realization particularly poignant is that I was quite sure there had been nothing in particular wrong at the time. It was just an everyday face. Then I realized that if the camera had captured this face then probably others were seeing it too, even if I'd rather they didn't.

So I decided to check it out. I proffered the snapshot. "Do I really look this way sometimes?" The answer from Wolf and the kids was, "Yes, that's a fairly common expression. Why do you ask?" Apparently they thought nothing of it. That face was just an everyday countenance to them. Unremarkable, familiar.

My worst fears confirmed.

On the one hand I was abashed to see the picture and to realize that this is what others were seeing day to day. On the other, it became an opportunity. (An AFGO!) Seeing this photograph in my twenties gave me a chance to become aware and have some influence over what was taking shape on my face.

I said to myself 'I better do something about this now.' I became aware of when I made 'that face.' I started paying closer attention to my facial expressions and catching grimaces sooner. I noticed my expressions when I was relaxed and when I was annoyed. I used the mirror now and then to see how what I was feeling was manifesting on my face. This intense attention only lasted a few weeks, but the awareness has endured.

Occasionally I think about that photograph when I catch a glimpse in the mirror of one of my drawn faces, brows furrowed, or lips pursed or narrow. I become aware of my feelings, my tension level, my judgments.

The issue reemerged into sharp focus again recently when my present husband, Mike said, "The expression on your face is ominous, Jill. You look like I have just said something atrocious. What exactly is going on?" I was taken aback, and couldn't imagine that it was as bad as that. I asked him to wait while I checked. I looked in the mirror and made the face I thought I had made. I was startled. It was forbidding. I agreed with him that the face he faced when he looked at me was way more grisly than the response I had meant to convey, which was just mild puzzlement and perhaps a bit of dissent. The expression of my face was as though I had just heard there was an axe murderer loose in our building. I could understand his alarm. Seeing the disconnect between how moderate inner upset showed on my face to others was instructive. My inner reactivity is invariably tied to past or future images. Simply becoming aware can bring me into present time.

In the now, things are invariably clearer and calmer than wherever else I might have been. Trying to avoid a draconian visage leads me to relax and soften in the moment. When my face and facial lines soften as a result of my awareness and relaxation, I feel it on the inside. Outer affecting inner. Being present to what is, rather than projecting or assuming, leads to a calmer, more relaxed expression. Inner affecting outer. It's a double, reflexive gift. A living, visual example of interconnection. Noticing my face as it appears on the outside and recognizing how it relates to my state inside is an ongoing opportunity to blend the physical with the spiritual. My face, its expressions, the way it manifests, comprise the anteroom of the temple that is my body.

There's a saying that the face we have before we turn 30 is the one we were born with, while the face we have after 30, we have, in some, ways earned. What happens day after day, year after year, on the inside will work on the face we were given at birth in not altogether unpredictable ways. We have some control over the shapes our mature face, and our body, will assume.

I am coming to terms with, and gradually accepting, my lines, the sags, my senior body and face. It was not always so. Until I was well into my fifties, when I met someone for the first time they were invariably surprised to hear that I had two kids in their thirties. I could see the mental wheels crank as they calculated how old I was. And they'd say something like 'Oh, I never would have guessed you were that age,' and this would give me an agreeable boost for the day. A tickle of satisfaction.

Sometime around 55, that changed. I noticed over time that no one said that anymore. No one was surprised at my age. The changes had taken their toll and my face was undeniably middle aged. The recognition sank in that there was nothing to do. This was the way things were. I experienced grief and loss that lasted for months. It was actually insightful to share this mourning with my grown children, to cry with them and then to laugh.

I went through an intensive period of considering cosmetic surgery. 'Just a little tuck here, a bit of a lift there. I have the money. It's not for others. It's just for me. It would give me so much pleasure,' I said to myself. And this may well be true for others. Each of us has to grapple with physical loss and changes in ways that seem appropriate. No one else can or should make these decisions. They need to come from deep inside us. And deep inside myself I knew that my route was acceptance and not surgery. I still think it would be nice to have the tucked and lifted face. I still hold my face the way it would look if the surgery were completely successful. I sometimes smile, then, and say to myself, 'This is the way things are now. Today.' And some days, it's not only what it *is*, it's even OK.

Some days I feel curious about the connection between my inner life and what I see on my face. About the lifting of my spirit

Becoming: Journeying toward Authenticity

and the mysterious spark that I feel when I look deeply, attuned to the wisdom and history visible in my own face and others'. Circles expanding. Looking into others' faces.

One other face in particular comes to mind. My husband's mother was a saint. Or as close as regular human beings come to one. She got to be almost 90 years old. We have several pictures of her around the house. Most of the time she is smiling. It's a warm smile that exudes kindness and good will. Even when she's not smiling, her face is warm and the lines are smile lines. The thousands of wrinkles convey ease, kindness, and internal well being to the on-looker.

I don't know, and don't need to know, all about Fran's inner life. It is sufficient and miraculous simply to truly see her. As I notice the richness and depth and character in Fran's face, my sense both of her and of me are transformed. We are connected by the witnessing, joined in a mysterious way. No longer just separate individuals. I am not just in my own world, contained, perhaps self-satisfied and aloof. When I observe, really look, give full attention to Fran, or even someone on the street as we pass each other, I feel the effect on my psyche. I am linked.

There is the other. And there is I. When we connect, even by just a glance, a momentary catching of eyes, there is a response. In that response there is a resonance. I am touched, changed, different. And the way I am changed, whether toward empathy and joining, or toward rejection and distancing, touches the other. They respond. It is a transformative dance.

When I can actually see, witness another's face, every other face—for every face in its own way is shining, unique, beautiful—this perception can transform. I transcend my daily routine, my semi-conscious status quo, my containment.

We now have ten grandchildren. Six of them under two, as I write this. Three barely a few months old. Looking into their faces I feel connected to a miracle, feel like I'm looking deep into being, partaking of and enjoying the separate manifestations of our ultimate oneness. Their faces are usually smooth, clear, soft, and yet distinct and each very different from the other. Unique. When the littlest ones scrunch their faces up with a concern, or gas, or fear, a myriad of forehead folds appear; crinkles emerge around their eyes that disappear again entirely when the trouble has passed and the smooth silk of baby skin is restored for the time being. Those crumples are delicate indicators of changes to come.

We all will, as will they, most assuredly, have more and more lines on our faces. I'd rather have smile and ease lines than the ones I saw on my some face forty years ago. And I'd rather be feeling ease and kindness than tension and anxiety. It's almost as though the lines are pathways... My face and yours are an intriguing journey, an inviting school house. So many different pathways, turns, lessons. More awareness. More learning. There will be more lines, and spaces. And opportunities. What will we make of them?

Related reading:
Campbell, Joseph (1968). *The Hero with a Thousand Faces.* Princeton: Princeton University Press
Lingis, Alphonso (1998) *The Imperative.* Bloomington, Indiana: Indiana University Press
Oliver, Mary (1986). *Dream Work.* NY: Atlantic Monthly Press

Reflections: *How do you feel about your face? What connections between your inside and outside worlds do you notice on your face, if any? What are some ways you experience others' faces? What emotions, feelings, judgments, thoughts typically come up? How do these affect you? How can the face be a window into deeper worlds?*

*"The mystery of life is not a problem to be solved,
but a mystery to be experienced."* Zen saying

*"Man's main task in life is to give birth
to himself."* Erich Fromm

૦ᐱᐑᐐᐤ

Purpose and Meaning

Related reading:
Berry, Thomas. (1999). *The Great Work: Our way into the future.* NY:
Random House
Frankl, Victor (1984). *Man's Search for Meaning.* Boston: Beacon Press
Schwartz, Tony (1995). *What Really Matters: Searching for wisdom in
America.* NY: Bantam Books
Smith, Huston (1982). *Beyond the Post-modern Mind.* NY: Crossroad
Publishing
Tolle, Eckhart (2005). *A New Earth: Awakening to your life's purpose.*
NY: Penguin Group

*"The lesson which life repeats and constantly enforces is
'look under foot.' You are always nearer the divine
and the true sources of your power than you think."* John Burroughs

*"If we are not totally blind, that which we are
seeking is already here. This is it."* Alan Watts

Look Where You Want to Go

One of my challenges and gratifications as I advanced undeniably into middle-age (and began, just as undeniably, to expand around the middle), was taking fitness instructor training and then a mountain biking course. A new life had brought me to Canada after long stints in the US and then in Europe. There were many uncertainties, many options, and no clear path or direction. How often do significant events in our lives grow out of 'chance' happenings that occur without foresight or planning...

It is a living example of 'how way leads on to way' as Robert Frost would have it. I hadn't been able to get to get a visa to live in Canada directly, but had been successful in obtaining a student permit. I needed to pick a degree, and Kinesiology sounded interesting. Taking a fundamentals of movement course led to discovering the fitness instructor's training. After completing that course, as one of the oldest participants, I became a volunteer instructor at the YWCA. After teaching class one day, I noticed a sign for a course entitled *Women's Only Mountain Biking*.

Now, my son Martin is a mountain biker. Crashing down hills, under brush, over rocks, flying though the air over precipices, all at a full throttle tear. Even big logs and stumps are no obstacle to mountain bikers. I had no ambition to come anywhere near such trails, or be around hard-core mountain bikers in action. But I had watched urban bike couriers, poised, waiting for a stop light to turn, standing upright, balancing gracefully on their pedals, making minute adjustments to their own and their bike's weight, scarcely moving and never touching down, then starting up smoothly when the light finally turned green; sometimes jumping curbs, with a slick little hop, up and onto the sidewalk.

So I signed up, clear that I'd leave the *real* mountain biking to crazies like my son!

When the course started, there were several first timers. Ellen, our instructor, after introductions and a first round of explaining gears and shifting, asked the repeat participants "What was the main, important lesson you got from the course when you took it the first time?" Silence. It had obviously not 'stuck' the way Ellen intended, so she said "Remember? It was 'Look where you want to go, not where you don't want to go.'"

It made a big impression on me from the get go. I immediately came to experience this maxim as crucial to mountain biking and cycling in general, but also saw its potential in more than just cycling. 'Look where you *want* to go, not where you *don't* want to go' has become a life lesson.

Our natural tendency is to look at what we want to avoid. In our effort to stay away from an obstacle, we actually focus on it. In the mountain biking course we were challenged to practice cycling slowly through mazes, for example, through the pedestrian gates that keep motorized vehicles off a path. As I approached the gates, my eyes were magnetically drawn to, literally mesmerized by, the barrier bars themselves. My bike veered toward them, and I had to put my feet down and stop. Trying again, I focused on the free space, which was where I *wanted* to go, where the wheel could pass through. Magically the bike went there, avoiding the bars, effortlessly passing the gate and emerging on the other side. I was dazzled, and remember the buzz as I experienced directly, in a simple but eminently practical way, the power of attention. I began to feel the insight, and its possibilities and opportunities, radiate out into many other dimensions of my life.

When we focus on something, give it our mental and emotional attention, it begins to grow and occupy more space in our lives. This is not rocket science, nor was it an entirely new concept.

Prior to this experience I had attended a number of silent meditation retreats in which I learned Vipassana, a Buddhist mindfulness practice. For the first time in my life I was invited, or rather advised, to sit still, pay attention and notice the way my mind worked. The retreats last for ten days, during which there is complete silence. No distractions. Not even reading or writing is allowed. There is hardly any choice but to pay attention to what's happening in your body and your mind.

On these retreats I experienced the 'monkey mind' so aptly described by the Buddhists, with its many dimensions and inexorable persistence. It darts about, pondering the past, flitting to the future, rarely resting, full of agitation, far from calm. Often my monkey mind went round and round in circles, drawn to, and obsessing about, things I was afraid of or disliked.

During one retreat, I was consumed by my frosted hair. My mind went spinning round and round, thinking 'If only the hairdresser had done a better job, I would look better, feel better, be better…' On the one hand I was mortified to see the pettiness of my focus. (Luckily I didn't have to tell anyone!) Yet it was illuminating to begin to observe my mental habits. There was nowhere to go, no one to talk to, so I simply had to observe, and be with, the patterns in my head.

On another retreat my mental focus was on relationship: 'If only he would do this, or be that, or maybe we could…' My mind was a merry-go-round, going over the same ground again, again, and yet again. I frequently discovered that I was focused on the negatives, the complaints, wishing something were different. My mind was inadvertently, habitually, unconsciously drawn to where I didn't want to go and that's exactly where I went. Over and over, in painful, useless, repetitive patterns.

As a result of these intense, mortifying sessions, I saw how familiar it was to focus 'where I didn't want to go.' Very gradually I began to learn to catch my obsessing, monkey mind a bit earlier when it began to circle around in a negative way. I could actually feel the tightening, the contraction, notice the narrowing of my consciousness as the spinning began. And with this awareness, the mental habits began to shift. There was more space, a slower pace, room to breathe and time to be present. I could start to notice where I was and where I wanted to go.

'Look where you want to go…' is just plain good advice when we're skiing, riding a bicycle, walking or driving along… Like Odysseus sailing between Scylla and Charybdis, avoid the whirlpools and beasts by focusing where clear passage is possible.

Metaphorically speaking, the phrase is also a simple and clever way to remember to keep our 'eyes on the prize.' It can help us make it through difficult times, pass an exam, or avoid junk food in a supermarket. Look where I want to go, not where I don't…

But this simple mountain biking maxim can also lead us wisely and well in and through deep spiritual terrain. One spiritual teacher speaks of 'two heaps' in our lives. One heap is the heap of ego matters: How am I doing? What do people think about me? Do I have enough? What shall I purchase next to try to be happy? Am I superior or inferior to that new person I just met? How can I cover up the deficiencies I feel?

The other heap is about our presence: What is happening now? What am I experiencing in this moment? Am I saying yes or no to the current reality? Can I accept what is?

The kicker is, of course, that the heap to which we pay attention is the one that will expand and develop. Normally we make this choice unconsciously, and it is by default and habit that we select the heap on which we will focus and spend the bulk of our time. We are usually run by our 'monkey minds' and occupied by the incessant and frequently negative prattle.

This is where the mountain biking maxim comes into play. When we can become conscious of where our minds are 'looking,' where our thoughts are drawn and our minds are hanging out much of the time, we can begin to shift where our attention lies, and thereby shift, so to speak, the relative size of the heaps. We can begin to grow in presence, take conscious breaths, look around us, begin to be here now—at least more often.

Thousands of years ago the Buddha said that what we are is the result of what we have thought. The mind is everything. What we think, we become. I am gratified at how age-old, profound Buddhist wisdom, conjoined with Ellen's modern, mountain biking guideline, inscribes increasingly larger circles, deepening and opening new directions and possibilities.

Related reading:
Almaas, A. H. *Two Heaps* (unpublished manuscript)
Chodron, Thubten (1999). *Taming the Monkey Mind.* Torrence, CA: Helan
Epstein, Mark (1995). *Thoughts without a Thinker.* NY: HarperCollins
Kabat-Zinn, Jon ((1994). *Wherever You Go, There You Are: Mindfulness meditation in everyday life.* NY: Hyperion
Ram Dass (1978). *Be Here Now.* Kingsport, TN: Hanuman Foundation

Reflections: *What does your mind do when you 'are not watching'? What does your mental chatter say? Whose voice is it? How large a chunk of you feels caught up in non-fruitful mental activity that keeps you from being present in the moment? Under what circumstances is it particularly challenging to 'be here, now'?*

*"Don't underestimate the value of Doing Nothing,
of just going along, listening to all the things
you can't hear, and not bothering."* Winnie the Pooh

*"We must learn to be still in the midst of activity and to
be vibrantly alive in repose."* Indira Gandhi

Just Do Nothing

D o you ever feel like the world is spinning out of control, or maybe wonder if it's you who is spinning, or out of control? In the middle of the spin it is hard to tell. Sometimes I get so busy 'doing' that I almost get dizzy. I've come to think that 'doing' can sometimes be like a disease: it takes me over and I'm not my usual self; it can be contagious, at times others want to stay away from me; the doing bug can be very persistent, insidious and hard to get rid of.

There are some of us who have a hard time getting started at all, and who may be particularly skilled at procrastinating. On the other hand, there are those of us who have a hard time stopping. Perhaps you may relate to all these parts, and find them active in yourself in different ways and times. I certainly do. This essay speaks to those of us, or that part of us, that 'can't stop.'

I am not referring here to the kind of constant activity and juggling that is required of single moms, people who hold down three jobs just to make ends meet, or those whose lives are in a phase (small children plus a master's degree on the go, for example). People in these situations have my full respect and support, and I'm not giving advice!

The 'doing' I'm talking about here is not the activity balancing that can be required in certain situations. I am referring, rather, to an inner quality, an addictive, compulsive doing, a frenetic, once-you-get-going-you-can-hardly-quit kind of activity. We read these days a lot about 'workaholics.' But that doesn't quite catch the quality to which I'm referring either. 'Do-aholic' seems more accurate. I like making lists and checking things off. (Sometimes I even write something on my list that I've already done, just so that I can have the satisfaction of crossing it off.) I used to meditate only in the morning because if I waited until afternoon I'd be so caught up in the spin that I wouldn't be able to sit still.

The need to do something often feels like an itch. An itch which seems to have a power all its own, driving the habitual, obsessive motoring, even when no doing is really necessary. I experience it as an internal agitation, a pushing feeling that says 'get on with it.' It is akin to frustration, a sand-papery experience on the inside that leaves no peace. I am used to overriding it in any of several ways. The easiest and most familiar strategy is to start doing and just not stop. Another way is to eat, or zone out. Sometimes even exercise (which is a relatively healthy habit, and I'm not knocking it), can be a way of avoiding or overriding the 'itch.' Each of us probably has our own particular strategy or set of them.

When I began to be curious and willing to inquire into the itch and the doing it generates, I was both alarmed and relieved when I had the insight that this incessant doing fills an internal emptiness. It seemed to be covering an abyss, an emptiness that at first seemed like a scary, gaping black hole. In the pit of the stomach, or taking up my whole core. No wonder we tend to keep busy. It means that we don't have to ask ourselves the questions about life, time, meaning, and existence that lurk in such holes.

What is more, the payoffs for 'doing' in our society are numerous and grand. So why stop, or even question it? We might think that if someone is busy, his or her life must be rich and full. Busy-ness can imply importance. And if someone is important, we should look up to him or her. Right? And often we do look up to busy people. Now, I am not disparaging people who are busy, people who accomplish small and large things. This essay is about what lies *beneath* the activity.

When we notice busy people, we rarely stop to ask what they're really doing and what drives or motivates them. In fact we can't actually do this for others. Yet it can be highly instructive to do it for ourselves. It took me years before I was sufficiently aware, and courageous, to ask myself these questions. I kept avoiding the exploration, rationalizing that it was 'just who I was, a do-er.'

Let me distinguish further between different kinds of 'doing.' For example, when I'm engaged in an activity that requires my full attention, I may be fully in a flow. I feel integrated and whole. This is not the busy-ness to which I'm referring. It's the other times, the frenetic, driven times, when I dart about, unfocussed, often allowing any little thing to distract me. I look for ways to shift focus, like checking e-mail every time something new comes in. Or I go in the kitchen to look in the fridge and snack on this or that. It keeps the doing going even if it's not focused, aware, intent. It's the spinning, avoiding sort of 'doing.' Caught in the act!

One extremely effective antidote can be to 'Just do nothing.' Slow down. Sylvia Boorstein says it even more explicitly in her book title: "Don't just do something, sit there." Break the pattern. Slow down. Get mindful. Notice the driver.

Ah, the driver. Once I took a course that included a personality test. I don't remember what the other three types were, I just remember that when I answered the questions I was dismayed to discover that my category was the 'driver.' I remember, too, when I took my first personal growth workshop, and we were given some feedback about how we affected others in the group, someone said about me, "You are a taskmaster, Jill. I wouldn't want to have to clean a room with you." Yes, I'd do a good job, and they might like to have their room cleaned *by* me, but they wouldn't want to clean it *with* me!

I remember the smart when I heard those comments. But also the surprise. I didn't know I appeared that way to others. There weren't even really any tasks to do in that workshop. How could they know what I was like when there was a job to be done? But they nailed it. And that same driver, taskmaster came out in the personality test years later. Still there, the old, familiar patterns.

A teacher with whom I was working at the time suggested, "Jill, why don't you take an hour a day and just do nothing." The thought really frightened me. But it seemed like a worthwhile challenge. Not to read, or meditate, draw, think, or not even to plan (one of my favorite escape activities). Just do nothing. I decided to give it a try. I could feel the inner resistance, the itchy internal agitation as I began my hour, so familiar is the focus on accomplishment to my ego. What about all the items on my list, the projects, the people I could be contacting, the letters to write, the activist stuff? Would people forget me? Would I fall down a hole, disappear? Would something dreadful (or wonderful) happen in the meantime that I would miss out on?

As I sit down on the couch, or out in the grass, for the setting is not important (it's possible to do nothing in the middle of a busy airport), and if I plunge down through the itch, the agitation, the fear, the emptiness, I feel the spinning start to ease. Almost like I imagine it might be when a dancer comes out of a pirouette. Slowing down. Starting to notice what's around me. Hear the sounds, sense the texture and smells of the environment. I begin not only to notice the external, but also my internal environment. I might still be able to recall and feel the agitation, the buzzy frustration that was overlaid by my usual activity. But if I persist, simply stay with my experience, I also become increasingly aware of the settling, easing, coming into the present moment.

And it wouldn't need an hour, either. Even those of us in the busiest of lives, or life phases, can take a moment to breathe, a second to look at who's in the driver's seat, a quick look at

Becoming: Journeying toward Authenticity

whether we are focused and present, or distracted and scattered. In a moment our worlds can shift, become more centerd and calm, almost like in the eye of a hurricane. It all begins with awareness.

Not that getting a job done is a bad thing. No superego attacks for this capacity. I can clean up, throw out, organize, make a space tidy and pleasant in a wink, see what needs doing and jump right in. Don't need to be told. And what is more, I like this about myself.

So what's the problem? Why all the fuss and prattle about busy-ness? It's because when I am spinning it is often a pointer to an imbalance, an inability to be present and a lack of consciousness. I am not in touch with myself, the world around me. I am simply not here, not in the present moment.

I used to believe that when I'd slow down (which is a little different from doing nothing, but related), I wouldn't get as much done. I have come to see that this is not true. There's actually a way in which I am more effective. When I'm spinning there's a hectic quality, a jumping from one project, idea or distraction to the next that often cancels out any authentic purpose or true productivity.

The moments of slowing down, of doing nothing, centering, dropping into the core, even if brief, are a form of regeneration, recreation, battery-charging. At such times I can feel the calming of the fear, the emptiness filling, being coming into its own, through and in me.

Related reading:

Almaas, A. H. (1998). *Facets of Unity: The enneagram of holy ideas.*
Berkeley: Diamond Books

Boorstein, Sylvia (1996). *Don't Just Do Something, Sit There.* San
Francisco: Harper Collins

Epstein, Mark (1995). *Thoughts Without a Thinker.* NY: HarperCollins

Huxley, Aldous (2004). *The Perennial Philosophy: An interpretation of the
great mystics, east and west.* NY: Perennial Classics, HarperCollins

Tolle, Eckhart (2003). *Stillness Speaks.* Vancouver, BC. Namaste Publishing

Reflections: *What are your strategies for handling yourself and the
situation when it seems like things are spinning out of control? When, if ever,
have you been someplace and intentionally done nothing at all? What is the
longest time you have ever been silent? What memories do you have of these
experiences? 'Who are you' when you are busy and 'who's at home' when the
center core is still?*

*"Your task is not to seek for love, but merely to
seek and find all the barriers within yourself
that you have built against it." Rumi*

*"The best and most beautiful things in the world cannot be seen or even
touched. They must be felt with the heart." Helen Keller*

Aligning with Love

L
ove is extolled by poets, tawdry and brilliant alike. For
songwriters it's a near ubiquitous theme. Scarcely a
bestselling book or film lacks a love interest. Mystics avow
that 'God is Love.' The Beatles sing 'All you need is love.' No
doubt about it, love is a biggie.

Over the years I have found myself beleaguered by doubts and
confusion, wondering if I know how to love, or if I even know
what love is. Rumi, the celebrated Sufi poet, refers to the barriers
that we construct within ourselves, and I have become increasingly
conscious of my internal obstructions to love. Sometimes it has
felt as though there is a yawning hole where my heart should be, a
hard knot in my chest, closed and defended. I have been alarmed
at times, and saddened, at the occasions and ways I am shut down,
numbed out and deadened, like a proverbial zombie. Looking
for access to love has seemed like trying to read a treasure map
written in secret code.

Part of the confounding around love is that the word has so
many meanings. In this piece I'm not considering 'in loveness,'
romantic love with sexual intimacy, as important as this topic and
experiences are. Being 'in love' is virtually living in an altered state:
we are aglow, we shine, and so does everyone and everything else.
I am appreciative of those periods in my life when I have been 'in

love.' But being 'in love' is not that against which I sometimes find myself inexplicably defended and have erected barriers.

Nor is the love about which I'm curious the deep, unquestioning love of devotees or disciples for a teacher or teaching. Devotion is a path that may give rise to profound devotional love. I respect that love and path, but that is also not the topic here.

So if not the in love of country songs and bestsellers, not the devotional love of monasteries and devotees, what other kind of love is there?

"...Faith, hope and love. But the greatest of these is love." Paul writes in his first letter to the Corinthians. This love is sometimes defined as "benevolent goodwill toward humanity; lenient judgment of others." Now there's a concept! And indeed, 'benevolent goodwill and lenient judgment' move toward the flavor of the love that I feel so often eludes me, and which is gravely contaminated by my inner structures and barriers.

Flashback: years ago I was on a B.C. ferry to Victoria for a training event. I looked around at my fellow travelers. They seemed distant, unfriendly, self-absorbed. I disparaged the books they were reading, the food they were eating. Each of them, and I as well, seemed isolated, separate, cold. It was physically and emotionally rather chilling.

After the seminar I returned to Vancouver on the same ferry. The passengers now seemed warm, connected, congenial. I noticed pleasant conversation, observed that most people were enjoying themselves and each other. There was inclusion and warmth that enveloped me and the whole ferry, and even seemed to extend far beyond.

Odd? Yes.

Impossible? No. It's a classic teaching that what we experience on the inside is what we perceive in the world outside. After the seminar I felt warm and open, so was inclined to notice what was warm and kind on the outside. It could have been a penetrating insight, but it did not sink in. I continued to struggle with my veils and barriers. Why were the world and I at times warm and benevolent, and at times harsh, isolated, inaccessible?

Flashback further: The care and attention I received from my parents was no doubt loving: I recall my dad holding me in his lap as I was a fat, little toddler, his reading to me; the way we played games and did puzzles together; my Mom's making mustard plasters for my congested chest, holding my hair back when I puked in the middle of the night, putting a cool washcloth on my forehead. We even got ice cream when we were sick!

While these experiences are clearly benevolent and caring, my experience of them was so inextricably intertwined with criticism, ambivalence, and hate (both coming toward me and emanating from me), that they seemed little help in illuminating 'the greatest of these.' How could love be so close to hate and still deserve to be called love?

But wait. Say it again (even though it seems ominous to utter the word). Hate. Love and hate are surely opposites. Maybe a reason I feel as though I don't know how to love is because I know so clearly that I hate. There are times I have hated my family, my partner, the people I have to work with, those who get in my way when I'm in a hurry, the bothersome folks who disagree with me...

Hate: I feel the blackness in my psyche, I want to destroy the object of my hatred, annihilate something, anything. It feels like lightning coming out of my eyes, zapping the person or situation. There's zing and zest in the experience, an energy that is empowering. Not warm and fuzzy, but definitely alive.

It's my growing experience that trying to stuff the hate (and pretending to feel sweet when the actual feeling is more like wanting to blow the person off the edge of the planet, sliver 'em into tiny ribbons and hang 'em out to dry), contributes to the numbing, the shutting down. Allowing the hate can actually blow that hole in my chest. Feeling (but not acting on) the hate is freeing, empowering, can create space. As I begin to embrace my hatred, I do experience that some of the barriers are breaking down.

Blocking hate can block love, but hate is clearly not love. And I'm still puzzled by the deadness, hardness, coldness I sometimes feel, even toward family and friends, those I'm closest to, and whom I am supposed to 'love' most deeply? I'm finding that my grandiose ideas about love are a further component of the predicament.

I discovered an unexamined assumption that the love for which I yearn is grand, pure, flawless. That it allows no stain. But look at me: I'm splashed with multi-colored stains. How could I be soft, open, 'benevolent toward humanity,' when I have a rock in my chest and judgments oozing out all over.

In a recent counseling session I experienced the possibilities. I was my usual self. Imperfect, full of mixed feelings. But as I settled, I noticed that my heart became accessible, I felt soft and open. What felt undeniably like love was not grandiose, it was a delicately human. Then my mind jumped in and scorned, 'But you couldn't function or be in the world that way. It wouldn't work. Love is perfect and you're not. You'd get dashed or dissolve into a pile of mush.' I decided to experiment.

After the session, I went out for a walk. It was dusk and the world was softly luminous. I felt connected to each person I passed. A mother and child were together on the beach. In my normal mode I would have just walked past, but with my openness, I connected with them, and together watched a sea otter cavorting in the surf. The little girl was ecstatic at the sight of the animal, but my thrill was at being able to be so open, so soft; to be in touch with the fullness of my heart, and still able to walk, talk, connect. I was full of kind regard, softness for the world and everything in it.

So the treasure was within reach. For me, imperfect, in the world. And yet connected to love, loving. The experience stayed with me for days, and is still a touchstone when I find myself hard, separate, stuck in my mind.

Becoming: Journeying toward Authenticity

I know in my heart that I care deeply for others, for their well-being; I am touched by kindness; by children, mine and others; by an insight, a shift, a piece of truth. At such times I smile inside, and outside, I relax and warm toward the people I pass on the street, and those close to me. Giving in to the isolation was not only making the world out there seem a dark and dingy place, it was limiting my capacity to live and give and care. Hiding behind the barriers was severely cramping and restraining me.

Holding both my frustrations (why should I love you when you don't love me?) *and* my goodwill, acknowledging my hardness (born out of past hurts and lingering judgments) while, *at the same time,* allowing my openness and kindness to be there as well. There's a path to love that I can walk. The treasure map I'd been seeking. When I first felt the possibility of both together, of barriers being there but not blocking access to the love, I was deeply touched.

It is possible. My limitations, the rock in my heart, *and* an opening toward the world, softness, receptivity. Again I find it's not this *or* that: love *or* hate and wariness, softness *or* hard defenses. I can experience and hold both, all, sometimes simultaneously.

It's especially heartening (pun intended) to notice that when I'm feeling frustration or anger, say toward my husband, recalling past hurts, bothered by the present, I can *also* experience kindness, softness. At the same time. When this first happened recently I teared up, noticing the expansion. Or take my kids. I know in my head and heart that I love them. And there were times when they were small, that I felt like knocking their heads together and locking them away, preferably in a deep, dark, dungeon! A mother-in-law, actually the saintly one in The Face, is known to have said, "No jury of women would convict another woman for murdering her children at 5:00 in the afternoon."

So love, yes, *and* hate, anger frustration… We can relish and welcome them all. And the greatest of these is love, *love, <u>love.</u>* It was there all the time.

Related Reading:
Dalai Lama, Jeffrey Hopkins, trans. (2005). *How to Expand Love: Widening the circle of loving relationships.* NY: Simon & Schuster
Jampolsky, Gerald (1990). *Love is Letting Go of Fear.* Berkeley, CA: Celestial Arts Publishing
Lewis, Thomas, Fari Amini and Richard Lannon (2000). *A General Theory of Love.* NY: Random House
Peck, Scott (1798). *The Road Less Traveled: A new psychology of love, traditional values and spiritual growth.* NY: Simon & Schuster
Welwood, John (2006). *Perfect Love, Imperfect Relationships: Healing the wound of the heart.* Boston: Shambhala

Reflections: *What is your relationship to love? Not to being 'in love,' but to common, everyday love. Name some ways that you discover love in your life. What is your experience of yourself when you are loving? What assumptions and beliefs do you have about love? How do they limit or expand your capacity to align with love?*

*"Who is rich? He that is content.
Who is that? Nobody."* Benjamin Franklin

*"Money frees you from doing things you dislike. Since I dislike doing
nearly everything, money is handy."* Groucho Marx

 ❧

Money, Money, Money

Does it make the world go 'round? Money has enormous energy. It's one of the hot and forbidden topics, along with sex and politics. 'Don't discuss these in polite society,' some say. Yet money is the subject of countless books, tapes, studies, and work groups. We debate and sometimes agonize over how to make more, attract lots of it, about how much is enough, how not to let it take over our lives. What is the link, if any, between money and a balanced life, a life of authenticity?

The very sound of the word sparks a charged emotional response in me. It's also a topic where my inner critic has been very active. For decades I felt inadequate about my capacity to make it. When I had gotten some, I felt guilty about that and struggled with how much to give away, how to be a good steward, how to invest in a manner that was congruent with my values.

As I was growing up, my parents didn't communicate clear guidelines as far as money was concerned. In fact we rarely mentioned money at all. It was considered gauche to talk about it, not good manners to mention money even in the family and certainly not in front of company. Both parents came from wealthy families and wanted their children to grow up believing that money was no issue. Even when it was. Although money was clearly important to them, there was never any explicit discussion about values, perspective, challenges in relationship to money.

I was about four when I received my first allowance. It was probably a dime, back in 1946. My allowance was never very much, even as an adolescent. Getting an allowance was supposed to be tied to doing some chores around the house, but even if I did a sloppy job on the chores, or forgot entirely, I usually could wangle the allowance.

In other families I know, where money was less rarified, parents gave their children substantial amounts of money to manage from the time they were quite young. Some children are given an allowance at a tender age and they are even supposed to buy clothes and school supplies, as well as have some spending money. What is more, in some cases there is no supervision at all. Kids were to learn the lessons about wasting, losing, and mismanaging early in life. The theory behind this approach is that it is a good thing to give children money early, that it cultivates a sense of responsibility. One dad tells how he watched and had to bite his tongue when his daughter spent all her money on a big plastic toy and candy when she had only shabby shoes and clothes.

I figure that both these parents and mine were trying to teach their children how to handle money well. Isn't that something we'd all like to know? I certainly would. How to manage money well... And for those of us who are parents, how can we teach our children this lesson, if at all? I certainly have no definitive answers but I have found sitting with the questions to be rich and provocative—an education in itself. What might it mean to 'handle money well'?

This question has many dimensions, and is hard to nail. But a clear counter example also sheds light. A colleague whose business it is to manage people's financial assets reported several instances of children having receiving a lot of money, (not an allowance of $1-$20 a week, but hundreds of thousands, or millions of dollars all at once) at a young age. He perceived that this basically ruined many of these young people and their lives. They didn't handle it well. And what exactly might that mean? To my colleague, it meant they began to live an excessive life style: they overspent, became more selfish and materialistic in their choices and values, and lost balance. In some cases this led to meaninglessness and suicide. It seems like 'handle it well' has something to do with balance and well-being.

So if having 'too much' money 'too early in life' can be a recipe for disaster, then we could ask 'Well, how much is enough?' My family clearly felt that we did not have too much. And sometimes not enough. I remember that it was considered a generous gift from my grandmother that I was able to go to summer camp. My parents were grateful and I wrote thank you letters to Granny for making camp possible. My family drove second hand cars, and lived in a house that was part of a fifties development. It was pleasant enough, perfectly adequate, but certainly not the kind of circumstances to which either of my parents had been accustomed. My parents thought they didn't have 'enough.'

When I told the story about summer camp to my first husband, who had grown up in Austria, during and post World War II, and used the example of my granny's gift to indicate that my family didn't have much money, he scoffed, "You have no idea what it was like to not have much money." His mother had knitted sweaters for her infants from unraveled wool garnered from cast offs from US soldiers, and walked many miles deep into the night to get a bit of milk from hill farmers to feed her children. Summer camp? Pure luxury.

Enough? The animalistic, instinctual part of us says 'Never enough!' It goes along with the ad I saw recently declaring, 'Less is never more. More is always better.' Studies show that no matter how much money people have, they rarely feel completely comfortable and secure. They always want about a third more than they already have. In our consumer culture we don't seem to have perspective on how much is enough. Handling money well will surely include developing some sense of 'enough.' And then being content with that. Accepting. Feeling complete.

Why is it some people have lots of money and others don't? Karma? Who knows? This is a mystery about which I have no clues. But it's clearly ripe for exploration.

Put your money where your mouth is? At times I have experienced great conflict over the lack of congruence in my investments and my values. There has been a loud-mouthed critic riding herd on me, sitting on my shoulder for decades, saying 'How can you pretend to be environmentally and socially conscious, and still let your money be managed in a way that at least in part flies in the face of these values? Bad girl. Shame on you!' So we can add 'congruence' to the list. The way I handle money needs to be congruent with my values and life priorities.

How do our attitudes and values regarding money relate to other parts of our lives? Spiritual teachings warn that money is dangerous. 'You can't serve both God and Mammon,' preachers often quote the Bible. My father always got gravely annoyed that the ministers used that in their sermons to pressure people to give lots of money to the church. That sent my dad packing and my family moved to another church. Is there any truth to the saying about God and Mammon? Where are our loyalties and how do we express them? How do we feel about the choices we make? Content, balanced, willing to share? Or conflicted, guilty, culpable…? Our feelings can be another clue to whether we are 'handling money well' or still have lessons to learn.

Can money actually be used and lived with in spiritual ways? Many modern authors maintain there is a way to hold and use money that is indeed congruent with a spiritual life. The reading and inquiry I have done around money gives reason to harbor some hope that this is true. Cautiously I would say it is slowly coming to be that way for me. Yet I think there are no universal answers. Only individual ones.

What about the connection between money and happiness?

Becoming: Journeying toward Authenticity

Numerous international and cross cultural studies show that once basic needs are taken care of, money has very little to do with whether people are happy or not. There are plenty of people with lotsa moolah who are gracious and generous, and plenty who are miserly and miserable. And the same thing is true for those in 'poverty.'

For many people money is inextricably related to security, to value, to self-esteem. There has been very little time in my life where I have fully supported myself financially. I went from being dependent on my parents, which carried on through university (oh yes, I had a few summer jobs and won a scholarship, but I could not have gone to university without my parents' help), to an early marriage where we were a partnership. We worked hard, and lived within our means, but before long, it was my husband who was supporting the family. I always helped a bit financially, but had lingering concerns that I might not have the means or capabilities to take care of myself and the kids if something were to happen to breadwinner dad. The key point here is that my not earning much money, not contributing financially, led to a lower sense of personal value, and to self-esteem.

Had I put 'making more money' as a higher priority, I may have done things differently. I made my choice to work part time, for a pittance, and have free time and time for my children. These are fine choices. What's not fine is that I was discontent and my self-esteem suffered as a result of not making 'enough' money. More important than making more money in my situation would be to have acknowledged and accepted the priorities I had, and to feel OK about my choices. In retrospect I would not have done it differently, but would like to have worked through the psychological and spiritual obstacles sooner and with more awareness. That didn't happen then. The topic of this chapter is a work in progress for me. How about you?

So we have balance, congruence, well-being, acceptance, and contribution as factors probably connected to 'handling money well.' This is a start.

Related reading:

Kinder, George (2000). *The Seven Stages of Money Maturity: Understanding the spirit and value of money in your life.* NY: Bantam Books

Needleman, Jacob (1994). *Money and the Meaning of Life.* NY: Doubleday

Nemeth, Maria (1999). *The Energy of Money: A spiritual guide to financial and personal fulfillment.* NY: Ballantine Books

Twist, Lynn (2003). *The Soul of Money: Reclaiming the wealth of our inner resources.* NY: W.W. Norton

Wilder, Barbara (1999). *Money is Love: Reconnecting to the sacred origins of money.* Longmont, CA: Wild Ox Press

Reflections: *How would you describe your relationship to money in your early years? How has it evolved, i.e. what is your monetary autobiography? What is your comfort level and where are your areas of conflict or distress in financial matters? What have you learned and what would you still like to explore in this area?*

"The happiness that we seek depends on our ability to balance the ego's need to do with our inherent capacity to be." Mark Epstein

"Simplifying our lives does not mean sinking into idleness, but on the contrary, getting rid of the most subtle aspect of laziness: the one which makes us take on thousands of less important activities." Matthieu Ricard

$\infty\sim$

If at first you don't succeed

… try, try, again, the saying goes. And my early life involved a great deal of trying. A lot of trying very hard. I tried hard to stand, walk, feed myself, get my parents' attention, to have them love and approve of me, have them give me candy and ice cream; I tried to ride my bicycle, please my teachers, get 100 percent on spelling tests. I tried not to lose my mittens on the way home, to stay out of trouble. Trying, and trying hard was just what you did. Mom said it, Dad said it. The world reinforced it. As a child, there seemed no other way to live each day but to try and try some more.

And at this young stage putting energy and effort into whatever seemed to bring smiles and good feelings, both within and without, certainly does make sense. We are learning to survive and to make our way, to grow up and get along.

Effort, focus, endeavor are important, so where's the rub? It's the lack of balance and the misplaced motivation for all the trying that burden and betray us and ultimately backfire.

Much of my efforting, for much of my life, was rooted in the need to please others, and the unconscious belief that my value as a person, as well as many of the important things in life, were sourced outside me, and could only be obtained by doing, trying, accomplishing. And these beliefs were often coupled with a fear of not measuring up, not being 'successful.'

When I recall all the trying from today's vantage point, I also remember the crying that came from trying: the ache, the exhaustion. It was not acceptable just to stop, to give up, to quit, to hate what you were doing and throw it against the nearest wall and smash it to bits. In the early days there was little room for thoughts of this nature, or acknowledgment of such feelings. Life seemed, at times, like a daunting set of tasks, and I was pretty well on my own. The trying, efforting, and endeavoring had a desperate, urgent and relentless quality.

The matter and degree of attachment are also important. We're usually clear about what we think we want or need, and quite desirous of getting it. Spiritual teachers talk about the agony and suffering of attachment and desire. I recall this suffering well, but knew no other options at the time, nor did I see the connection between this form of trying and suffering.

So the 'trying' continued. Maybe you can sense the flavor of the exertion. Perhaps it smells and tastes familiar. As an adolescent I tried to be included, not to stand out awkwardly, to get high marks on tests but not be a nerd, to have a best friend, to have a date to the prom. I tried not to get caught sneaking cookies, not to be seen eating alone in the cafeteria, to keep from getting too fat. I tried to look at ease and cool when I didn't feel that way, to make interesting conversation, to be independent without being lonely. I was frantic to feel good about myself and knew no other dependable way except by trying.

Of course there were sweet moments. Softer times. Larger glimpses. Cracks in the armor. There were afternoons of tea with friends, moments where I was not doing anything that could be deemed fruitful or productive. But not many. Even reading was about becoming educated, to build vocabulary; exercise was to get slim and healthy. There was an undertone that hummed the importance of trying your hardest.

And in today's world the active life gets frequent and affirmative press: action is the way to health and vitality, to happiness. Plus it would save our health care systems lots of money! Get active, stay active, think active, try, try, try…do, do, do. In many circles there is no reflection on endeavor: making an effort is always good. Our hyperactive, materialistic society tells us in pictures and words that glory can be gained if we run toward the possibility of success.

Panning back to look at a larger picture, we may perhaps perceive a subtle twist. While being active in the world *is* indeed part of a full life for many people (and I am not minimizing or discarding the value), we can actually stay healthier, function more effectively, (and save our health care system money!) when we act from a deep, still place rather being driven by the surface hectic. But for decades I had absolutely no awareness of this possibility.

Simply 'being' was not something I knew or learned about. Even a moment can make a world of difference. But it was neither praised nor regarded. Stillness received no mirroring or acknowledgment from my parents, teachers or caregivers. No one ever said, "How nice it is to see you just sitting still, being quiet. Paying attention to your breathing, noticing your inner body, you're touching into the source of all that is. Being and awareness will stand you in good stead in your life." Unthinkable! Efforting was drummed so loudly that it usually drowned out other, softer tones and melodies.

What are the emotional and psychological consequences of all this efforting? How does it affect our consciousness, our souls (not to mention the planet)? For me (and for a long time), the ongoing trying tended to reinforce the familiar ego groove in my psyche asserting that my value as a person comes from doing, not from being.

Even as I say this, a familiar part inside me pops right up and confirms the traditional view, saying 'It's right, one should never give up. Keeping at it really *is* important.'

And doubtless, there is some merit to this. Such issues are rarely simple or straightforward. I recently saw a film on brain functionality that emphasized the importance of perseverance, even in the face of indomitable odds. For example, a brain injury leaves someone with scarcely any capacity for movement. Well guess what? People recover from these injuries by the sheer force and dint of will, by trying and trying again. So it is clear that there's a time and a place for sheer struggle, goals and endeavor, not giving up. Again, we come to the notion that it's the lack of balance that is damaging and deadly. This imbalance coupled with the belief that we are the ones doing it, that we're doing it alone, that we're in charge.

There is even a form of spiritual efforting as well. Trying doesn't necessarily disappear or soften when we expand our horizons. Some days right now when I get up out of bed in the morning, I resolve: to be productive, to get things done, to be a good person, to be considerate, to pay attention, to remember to sense my arms and legs, to evolve in consciousness…

Eee gads. Here it goes again! What a mountain to climb! We've raised our sights but are using the same weapons. Where's the exit? How do I escape? Or can *I*?

When we look precisely at *who* is trying, usually we will find the ego personality at core. At the root of the kind of efforting that is exhausting—lonely, with no place to rest, underscored by the pressure to be someone, to accomplish, even to serve, to pick ourselves up and give it another whack—we often find a deficient ego.

Even if the surface trappings look good, all egos, deep down, are partly fearful and insecure. The good and bad news is that sometimes we all act from this place. It's universal. Not a shocking thing. Completely natural. We all have an ego structure, we all are at its mercy much of the time. We feel pushed, driven, trapped, and we do our best. Not to knock it. No reproach. Just curiosity… But there is something else we might find if we keep exploring.

When we look more closely, we can discriminate a form of trying that can be fun and interesting, worthwhile in a larger sense. In the exertion, learning, developing a sense of mastery, there can be a looseness, an ease, a quality of giving up, which used to be anathema, but is now a kind of freedom.

Yes, there are bills to pay, kids to educate, decisions to make, busses to catch. If we take our actions toward these tasks from the place of ego deficiency, lack of acceptance of the present moment, we are bound to suffer. But consider this: the same invoice, the same F on the test, the same bus, caught or missed, if accepted, can be a teacher, an opportunity for a deep breath, coming to ourselves, getting present, or beginning again, as Zen teachers say.

I believe we are beginning to mature when we begin to recognize the place and time to surrender, when we come to accept what is, and to let go of our usual ego efforting. It's possible for the doing to arise, not from the deficient, pushing place in our selves, but from a depth and alignment with our stillness at our core. Ego tries. Presence flows. We can take a breath, come to ourselves, and then do what seems appropriate and called for in the situation. Bills, busses, tests, decisions. The actions taken from acceptance might not even be very different: we might still sit down to study, look for an additional job, take a cab or cancel an appointment. But the difference in our experience is radical. A world of difference.

Related reading:
Brahm, Ajain (2005). *Who Ordered This Truckload of Dung? Inspiring stories for welcoming life's difficulties.* Boston: Wisdom Publications
Epstein, Mark (1998). *Going to Pieces without Falling Apart: A Buddhist perspective on wholeness.* NY: Broadway Books
Lau-Tsu (Stephen Addis and Stanley Lombardo, trans.) (2007). *Tau Te Ching.* Boston: Shambhala
Thomas, William (2007). *What are Old People For?: How elders will save the world.* Acton, MA: Vanderwyk & Burnham

Reflections: *What is your attitude toward trying hard, endeavoring to accomplish goals? What effect has the efforting had on your body and psyche? Is it possible to notice who is trying, who cares about the results? What is your ego afraid would happen if you didn't try in the familiar manner? What would it be like to be still for a while when you feel a need to make yet another effort?*

Becoming: Journeying toward Authenticity

*"After the game, the king and the pawn
go into the same box."* Italian proverb

*"When one door closes another door opens; but we so often look so
long and so regretfully upon the closed door, that we do not see the ones
which open for us."* Alexander Graham Bell

Success

In the essay on Trying, we didn't explore in any depth what success might actually mean. And indeed, for years I had no definition. Success was simply something 'out there,' unquestioned, something for which one was to strive. The message was omnipresent; nearly everyone in my world thought success desirable, important, worthy of much effort.

But what is it that we're calling 'success'? If we track the evolution of what success might mean over the course of a lifetime we might find that as a young person, success means simply surviving. Much of our lives are spent adjusting, learning how to be a functioning individual, developing structures and capacities that will allow us to be human beings that can get along in the world. And we all 'succeed' in this, to a greater or lesser degree.

In my family, there was an underlying sense that almost every moment could be improved upon, learned from, optimized. 'Success' had a flavor of mastery to it, becoming more capable and continuing to develop skills. Later this acquisition of capacity morphed to include a future focus: success involved 'making it,' getting into the right schools, finding the right, prestigious path... There was an underlying urgency, a sense of grit and fortitude attached to the notion. In my early days there was not much tolerance or acceptance of weakness or faltering.

To some, success means fame and glory, riches and recognition. No wonder. We are encouraged in magazines and on television to aspire to eminence and renown; we are exhorted to accumulate. Billboards and commercials spout the message; it is all but ubiquitous in our western culture. And these messages contain the implication that success will bring satisfaction and happiness. Sound suspicious? Limited, and also rather harsh and lonely? But this was the early reality for me, and I think for many of us in this culture.

At the same time, if we look around, we can also find radically contrasting views of success. Some actually hold in contempt the traditional markers of material success such as property and luxury, and go so far as to suggest that our measure of success corresponds directly to our disinterest in money, eminence, acquisition.

These views of success, whether in favor of, or opposed to, accumulation and fame, are both focused on what's happening outside of us. Reflecting on my experience, I recognize the hopelessness of trying hard inside with our focus only outside. Not only are the goals questionable and shifting, the path is fraught with frustration and doubt.

If we grant that it's not easy to find the key to success, what can we say about failure? Here's a sure key: try to please everybody. We are guaranteed to fail at that!

But there are other considerations here than just contrasting the two: success and failure. What about their interactions, their interconnection? Though it might appear counterintuitive, I find myself broadening and softening when I include the notions of 'failure' and weakness into my idea what success can mean. The picture begins to relax, expand, welcome otherness. We might even suggest that there is little wisdom in success. Our deeper learning, increases in our sensitivity and wisdom, come when we fall down, when we don't reach what we set our hearts on. We are not accepted into the school, job, club we thought we wanted; we have an accident or illness that thwarts our plans. Possibilities for learning, acceptance, compassion, creativity emerge. Successes of another nature.

George Washington Carver invites us to take in the larger picture of humanity as we travel along the path. "How far you go in life," he suggests, "depends on your being tender with the young, compassionate with the aged, sympathetic with the striving and tolerant of the weak and strong. Because someday in life you will have been all of these."

In our exploration of the meanings of success we've moved outward to include a large spectrum of humanity, and we can also move inward to consider an entirely internal notion of success. Success, some say, is found not in the applause of the crowd or through other forms of external acknowledgment, whether financial or material, but rather in having done our best regardless of outcome; this deep feeling of personal satisfaction and contentment indicates success.

There are other views of success that focus more on what's happening inside rather than what is visible outside. If we love what we do, some say 'the money will follow,' but it may or may not. Yet some people feel successful if they are doing what they love, regardless of the magnitude of external rewards. Being at peace with ourselves will be the satisfactory definition of success for some.

Others would have us add components of service, expanding the definition of success to include our relationship to others. If a life comprises qualities such as sincerity, personal integrity, humility, courtesy, wisdom, charity, some would call this life successful.

Continuing to look inward, and including others in our circle, we may come to question the motivation of our exertion. For whom and for what? Again, we find deeper, richer options. If we are striving to be beneficial and kind, or we are seeking wellbeing for ourselves, others, or for the planet, it is the direction that matters, not whether or not we achieve a particular goal or not.

For some the principles that encourage us along our way and inspire us are what matter. Lives lived in alignment with ideals such as truth, goodness, beauty, service to others, to some this is success.

We can attain some perspective regarding the complex and perplexing notions of success by remembering that although no one can go back and make a brand new start, anyone can start from now and make a brand new ending. All things change, flow, slip away, but we can always begin again, afresh, right where we are.

There need be no agreement on what success means, or the purpose of life, or what it means to have lived well. Each of us will seek and find our own answers, and they will likely evolve and transform over time.

I have come to rest with this notion of success offered by Sister Corita Kent: "Love the moment. Flowers grow out of dark moments. Therefore, each moment is vital. It affects the whole. Life is a succession of such moments and to live each, is to succeed."

Related reading:
Dalai Lama et al (1992). *Worlds in Harmony: Dialogues on compassionate action.* Berkeley: Parallax Press
Eber, Dorothy ((1991). *Genius at Work: Images of Alexander Graham Bell.* Halifax, NS: Nimbus Publishing
Thich Nhat Hanh (1992). *Peace is Every Step: The path of mindfulness in everyday life.* NY: Bantam Books

Reflections: *What does success mean to you? Where did this notion come from? How did it happen that you took it on? To what degree does the concept of success make a contribution to your life, and in what ways does it detract? What about 'failure': is there such a thing? What does it mean to fail? How are success and failure related, if at all?*

"There ain't no answer. There ain't gonna be any answer. There's the answer." Gertrude Stein

"Our life is a faint tracing on the surface of mystery." Annie Dillard

∿∿

Shadows and Ambiguities

Related reading:
Dillard, Annie. (1999). *For the Time Being.* NY: Penguin Putnam
Giesel, Theodor (1971). *The Lorax.* NY: Random House
Goleman, Daniel (1995). *Emotional Intelligence.* NY: Bantam Books
Korten, David (2006). *The Great Turning: From empire to earth community.* Bloomfield. CT: Kumarian Press
Krishnamurti, J. (1969). *Freedom from the Known.* NY: HarperCollins

*"It is not our differences that divide us. It is our inability
to recognize, accept and celebrate those differences." Audre Lorde*

*"We may have come over on different ships but
we're all in the same boat now." Martin Luther King Jr.*

೧೨೮

In or Out?

"Are you an X or an O?" we were asked. I was at a workshop
during an Association of American Wives of Europeans, an
AAWE conference in Paris. The attendees were all women,
from various backgrounds and living in different countries. One
woman spoke of being the only Caucasian in an Arab school.
Another of being Russian Orthodox in the Canadian farm town.
Yet another recounted the first time a black person came into her
Austrian village. Each of us brought to the workshop a unique
set of associations, hopes and fears about inclusion and exclusion.
As I heard their stories I was drawn back in time to the throbbing
twinge of adolescent exclusion.

In the junior high school where I grew up, social clubs were
a large part of the scene. Those who belonged to these clubs
seemed to me to have a confident way of walking and talking,
they laughed together, and met after school. They exuded an
exclusive sense of belonging, and I wanted in.

Even if you were accepted into one of the social clubs, there
were the truly 'in' clubs, highly desirable ones, and the 'out' clubs,
for those who didn't make the first cut. Or that's the way it
seemed to me. And then there were those kids who received no
invitation at all, not even to a second tier club. That seemed to
me like being labeled an outcast, or branded as unacceptable—a

terrible fate, something akin to death.

And there was no way to will yourself into the group you wanted to belong to. Not taking no for an answer was not an option. No sense of entitlement would guarantee that you would survive the selection process. Many were invited to the first parties, few were asked back. I was elated to receive a first invitation to an 'in' club. I spent hours agonizing over what to wear to look my best to make the finest possible impression. I waited in the family room on the Saturday afternoon of that first party for one of the club members to pick me up. The gray wool of my bermuda shorts, carefully selected by my mom and me, slightly scratched my skin. My mom was vicariously and painfully involved in the social events of her children. She and I had fretted about the shorts, the knee-high socks and black top. In the end, my mom and I decided that the outfit went well together, that it made me look smart and stylish.

During the party, I tried my hardest to be entertaining, to smile enough but not too much, to talk enough and be clever but not brash. Having a good time was not something that concerned me much. I wanted to be liked and accepted. At this time in life my self-worth came almost exclusively from the outside, from the approval of others.

After that first party, I waited and waited, but no second invitation arrived. I remember the sting of the waiting, the rejection, the longing. There was nothing I could do to 'make it happen,' to be accepted into club A. It was small consolation that the members of a club B liked and wanted me. Club B was not an 'in' club. I was very attached to the outcome: Club A and not club B. That's what I wanted. It would be decades until I even heard of 'non-attachment,' and the teaching about the pain associated with desire and attachment. But when I did, I would have much experience to draw on! I felt this suffering viscerally in the seventh grade, but had no larger context or holding for the pain.

Of course I got by. The girls in club B were lovely, warm, inclusive, and at times manipulative, catty and cutting. It was a typical group of mid-west, north American teen-age girls. It would not have been different in club A. But the wounds of the process and rejection were deep, and I continued to feel them for decades.

It might seem as if I am entirely focused on myself, as if I lack concern about how others experienced in- or exclusion. Indeed, how often does it happen that we are part of a majority, say of Xs, and just don't consider what it might be like to be an O? The questions have individual and personal, as well as community and world cultural, implications. It can be both humbling and enriching to notice how the many ways of being included or excluded, or of including and excluding others, affect us and ripple out to affect others.

It is in part the pain I experienced in my adolescent years that has led me, as an adult, to receive stories of inclusion or exclusion, among them those of the AAWE women, with greater curiosity and compassion. It is in part because I was in club B in junior high that I pay closer attention to both Xs and Os, to the manifold processes by which we include and exclude. At least during the better times when I remember to pay attention at all!

Related reading:
Belenky, Mary, et al (1986). *Women's Ways of Knowing: The development of self, voice, and mind.* NY: Basic Books
Kingsolver, Barbara (1998). *The Poisonwood Bible.* NY: HarperCollins
Mindell, Arnold (1995). *Sitting in the Fire: Large group transformation using conflict and diversity.* Portland, OR: Lao Tse Press
Schaef, Anne Wilson (1992). *Women's Reality: An emerging female system in a white male society.* NY: HarperCollins
Thomas, William (2007). *What are Old People For?: How elders will save the world.* Acton, MA: Vanderwyk & Burnham

Reflections:
What role has inclusion and exclusion, being 'in' or 'out,' played in your life? How does it manifest in your culture? Recall a situation where you were excluded and one where you were the excluder. What would you do differently in these situations, if anything, if you had known what you know now?

"Three things in human life are important. The first is to be kind. The second is to be kind. The third is to be kind." Henry James

"If we had no faults, we would not take such pleasure in pointing out other people's." LaRochefoucauld

Judgment, Curiosity, and Compassion

Unconsciously, naively, I had absorbed the metaphor of life as a battle between good and evil from very early on, at home, at school. I saw this struggle exemplified in many arenas: on the political scene, in the news, around my neighborhood, in my own family. There was an undertone that assumed the existence of polarities: right versus wrong; good and bad, us versus them. My family was inclined to give some credence to conspiracy theories. From my parents I heard about the dangerous communists and their sympathizers who threatened 'freedom loving people' all over, especially in the USA.

Judging was second nature to me. I habitually evaluated others and also myself. It seemed a rational and dependable way to know you were on the right track: assess and compare yourself to others and thereby check out whether you were doing OK. It had a neat, comfortable and reassuring predictability to it. I knew just what to do with a new view, a different perspective, another way of looking at the world. I'd ask, 'How does it compare to what I do and know? Is it better or worse?' As a result of this early exposure to the perspective of opposing forces I tended to see the world in black or white, without many shades of grey.

What is more, the judging-evaluating habit could create a bit of a high, and definitely had its payoffs, including the possibility of

Becoming: Journeying toward Authenticity

feeling righteous, superior, and confident, at least in the moment. The poignant thing was, I didn't even know I was doing it. I didn't even think about it. People, places, ideas, values, habits... all got compared and evaluated. It never occurred to me that there was another way to be, think, or process new information.

Not that I would be overtly rude or contrary in the face of difference, or that I would act out my judgments in a blatant way. But they were stored inside, and were part of the ranges of comparison that comprised my inner landscape.

Then one evening, long ago, a high school friend, responding to some evaluative pronouncement of mine, said to me, "Jill, have you not heard the biblical admonition that we should 'judge not, lest ye be judged'?"

Now I had done some bible study, and knew about the ten commandments and the golden rule. But Lydia's counsel, deep and classic and compelling, long ago on that memorable evening, and which caught me at a moment bursting with adolescent posturing, hadn't registered on my psyche. Judge not. I was taken aback by Lydia's comment. But how was one to know what to say or do if not by evaluating and judging? What about good and evil, right and wrong, and telling them apart?

Indeed, what about them? I didn't respond to Lydia at the time but these questions whirled through my head that night and long thereafter. A seed had been planted. It would lie rather dormant for years, but I had begun to wonder. Some slight shred of doubt had been cast on my formerly iron-clad habit of mind.

I remember several milestones, inner and outer, which have invited and encouraged me to move toward responding to people, situations, and ideas with curiosity and compassion instead of judgment and evaluation.

One involved reassessing one of my well-worn mental strategies. Well into mid-life, after reading books on psychology and beginning to do some spiritual and inner work, I gradually became conscious about a strategy that I had used for decades to bolster my ego. It was unnerving to discover that my tactic actually involved comparing myself to others across a whole range of performance criteria. Using the notion of a normal distribution bell curve, I mentally pictured my rank in comparison to others. I could accept that some people were clearly smarter, richer, more beautiful, more environmentally responsible, better parents, more fit, more socially active than I was. That was obvious. (And this is by no means an exhaustive list. My list of my criteria went on and on. There was no end of ways to rank myself, judge others, feel inferior or superior.)

Here's how the strategy continued. As I pictured the bell curves, I then told myself that while there were others who were 'better' than I was in all those various categories, I was also 'better than' a whole host of people as well. This exercise was oddly comforting and deeply familiar. I usually wound up feeling that I was not doing too badly, which of course was the goal of my patterned personality: artificially to pat myself on the back; to feel, if not exactly superior, then at least good enough.

Learning more about my habit of judging and comparing has also led me to see the damage my inclination had on relationships. It affected my ability to be present, really to be myself and to let others be who they were in the moment. I was living out of past experiences and projecting them onto the present. Often they veiled the possibilities of the moment. If I were feeling excluded or isolated, (an example of an early experience), I would tend to see others as doing this to me, excluding me, not wanting to have me around. I might respond in a defensive manner to a harmless comment, or might not step forward for fear of being rejected. If I were an X, I might well feel excluded by Os, rather than being comfortable as an X and curious about what it was like to be an O.

Krishnamurti once said that a great contribution to inner peace lies in 'not minding how things are.' When I first heard this it struck me like a gong. It was clear from the context that

Becoming: Journeying toward Authenticity

he didn't mean we should be so detached as to be distant or uncaring. It wasn't about withdrawing. I began to experience a glimmer as I realized it meant that we can find peace by accepting what is from a positive, active, probably even often a grateful place. What a sweeping contrast to judging and evaluating.

Here's how it could play out in everyday life. I might want to plan a get-together with my family and invite my daughter and her children. Say it turns out that my daughter declines because she wants to take some time for herself. When I 'don't mind what is,' I accept this, needn't feel 'excluded,' or feel bad thinking I was insensitive to ask. It's just what is in present time. An invitation was declined. That's the way it is, and it's OK. What freedom!

As this approach became more understandable, it also became quite gratifying: when I stop playing the right or wrong, blame and judgment game, and begin instead to get curious, I feel my heart open. My face softens and I can sense the softening within, as well. It's like I'm being caressed by a gentle hand. The tension flows away from my eyes, my cheeks and jaw. And the situation becomes more spacious, gracious, fluid. Compassion may arise, for myself and others, for what's happening on the planet, for the human condition. Maybe humor and lightness. What a trip. You just never know what's next.

This deep-seated tendency to judge and evaluate others and myself is just one of many patterns I've noticed in my ego structure. The exploration of these structures, and chunky, clunky places is a lifetime path. Begun, but never done.

Only recently have I understood how judging and comparing can lead on to griping and complaining, and how that can lead to bad chemistry in one's body, maybe to migraines, or overeating... The mind-body connection works in mysterious ways. Another interesting thing about complaining. While it's truly effortless to do when we're discontent and irritated with what's happening, it's completely useless. Nothing comes of it except ill-will and bad energy. When we can do nothing about it, complaining is like shouting at the wind, entirely pointless. Actually worse than pointless. Shouting at the wind might well get one's physical energy flowing, while complaining about something we cannot change gets bad chemistry flowing.

Taken together, complaining and judging create quite a devastating team. I recently was inquiring into my passionate commitment to environmental issues. I noticed how I tend to complain and gripe about the state of the world, polluters, abuse of corporate power, greed, exploitation. (You know the sort of list I mean. You probably have your own, in whatever areas are of particular concern to you.) Then I felt into the judgments that grew out of the complaining mindset: 'How could they? Aren't they despicable? And aren't I the noble crusader to try to right some of these wrongs?' It was almost deafening, the mind chatter, all about making me the good one, putting others on the dark side. Bolstering my ego, demonizing my perceived opponents.

As I got deeper into the exploration I noticed how separate I felt, how the complaining led to judging led to isolation, even to powerlessness, and that in fact part of my judging was to cover up my own felt lack of power. What would it be like, I wondered, to own my own power and capacity, and to take action from strength and compassion instead of as the angry victim riddled with complaints and judgments?

This turned out to be a revolutionary question. As I felt into that possibility I grew large and soft at the same time. Full of capacity and good will, but lacking in harshness or hopelessness. My actions, (writing activist letters, disseminating information to encourage others to act), might well be the same. But writing them, I was no longer a small, separate, bitter person suffering from PLOM (poor little old me) disease, rather I was an individual, yet part of a larger whole. Acting in a flow, surrendering the burden of responsibility, and the painful personal attachment to the outcome, becoming part of a larger enfoldment. Often there is not even any particular outcome, rather an ongoing process of which this person I am in this moment is a unique part.

What a transformation.

It has been exciting and challenging, scary and humbling, to bring the light of awareness to the nooks and crannies where the ego's habits lurk. The rewards have been great and I feel gratitude for the changes I've noticed in recent years. It's lovely when a friend comments that I seem softer, a colleague mentions how clear I look, how at ease and comfortable I appear in the training situation, how I seem less hectic and more confident. The inside rewards are sufficient, but it's a sweet bonus when becoming more real is apparent to others as well. Gravy, so to speak.

Related reading:
Chodron, Pema (1997). *When Things Fall Apart: Heart advice for difficult times.* Boston: Shambhala
Chodron, Thubten (2001). *Working with Anger.* Ithaca: Snow Lion Press
Hopkins, Jeffrey (2001). *Cultivating Compassion.* NY: Broadway Books
Jampolsky, Gerald (1990). *Love is Letting Go of Fear.* Berkeley, CA: Celestial Arts Publishing
Sarno, John (1998). *The Mindbody Prescription: Healing the body, healing the pain.* NY: Warner Books

Reflections: *What role does judging and evaluating have in your life? What is the flavor of some of the judgments you absorbed during your childhood? What effects do they have on you today? How does your ego typically bolster itself? When and how did you become aware of these patterns? What could be in the space if the judgments were absent?*

*"Truthful words are not beautiful, beautiful words are
not truthful. Good words are not persuasive, persuasive words
are not good. He who knows has no wide learning, he who has
wide learning does not know." Lau Tzu*

"What is to give light must endure burning." Viktor Frankl

The Road to Hell

… is paved with good intentions, states a familiar proverb. My experience with this maxim contains both wisdom and pain.

The adage came alive for me one evening early in my spiritual work. I was with a like-minded group to meditate and explore the practice of inquiry. It was the dark time of year. The days were short. Winds whipped the soggy leaves, and heavy rain doused me on my way to the meeting, providing a west-coast wintry contrast to the warm sense of mutual support and connection I usually experienced as we sat gathered together. Inquiry is about waking up; it's called 'work,' and is a compassionate way of paying close attention to one's experience in the present moment. With curiosity and awareness. It often contrasts radically with my usual experience, in which I just drift along in my life, more or less unconsciously.

Jessica was there that evening. We did not know each other well, but we were both committed to the practice and the group. After the initial meditation, we began to inquire. I remember my excitement at the power of the practice, my desire to support people in this challenging work, and my enthusiasm for the learning and maturing that was taking place in others and in myself. I can sense even now my heart opening, the soft compassion, and the bit of excitement I felt as I commented on Jessica's work.

Becoming: Journeying toward Authenticity

Meaning to be helpful and respectful, I carefully summarized what I had heard her say: "So Jessica, what you sense is a contraction and deep hurt when you think about what happened last week, and that seems new and puzzling to you." Then, thinking she had completed her inquiry I asked, "I wonder if anyone else has comments for Jessica?" There was silence in the group. I concluded it was time to move on to the next person. Putting my relatively new facilitator's training into action, and my natural inclination toward inclusiveness, I said "Well then, who would like to work now."

I was completely unprepared for what happened next. Jessica began to shout and rage. Her face grew white and rigid in one moment and livid purple and wildly animated in the next. Her outburst lasted for several minutes. "You have no business telling me what I'm feeling! You're not in charge of this session! You're just like my mother! I can't believe this is happening! I feel sick. Won't you just shut up, or better yet, get the hell out of here."

As it turns out, Jessica was absolutely right. I didn't realize it at the time, but what I had done is quite inappropriate in the inquiry process. Understanding this, as well as dealing with the effect of Jessica's harangue and berating was a fascinating process and a massive learning experience. I see it now, years later in retrospect, indeed as an AFGO (Another Fricking Growth Opportunity).

In the moment, I caught my breath, and dribbled out something like, "I was just trying to make sure I understood you, and to see if there was anything more you wanted to add, and then I wanted to see that others got a chance..." "You don't get it, do you? You're not the facilitator here," Jessica burst in. My continued efforts to clarify what I believed to be my innocent and helpful intent continued to trigger her anger. To her, I had been out of line and was sabotaging the whole process.

The situation arose in the first place because the teacher of the inquiry group had set us out to sea with neither instructions on how to use the boat nor any directions on what to do if we encountered rough waters or ran aground. But that couldn't be helped at this point. Here we were, caught in a storm, without guidance and no rescue ship in sight. The other people in the inquiry group were untrained as well, and mortified at the uproar. We struggled through the rest of the evening, doing the best we could. But it was apparent that everyone was affected by the blow-up and having a challenge to reestablish a safe, respectful environment.

That evening at home, alone in bed, I reran the scenario in my brain, felt the turmoil and distress in my body, my heart racing, my limbs stiffening with anger and embarrassment. I didn't sleep or even begin to calm down for hours. I took comfort in my righteous sense of having had good intentions, and of being a gracious facilitator. I remember thinking, 'This is simply who I am. I want to clarify, check in, keep things running smoothly, be inclusive. Why did she get so upset?'

At about 2:00 in the morning, exhausted and drained, I decided to call my husband, who was out of town at the time. I spoke about what had happened earlier that evening, and ran through it my mind yet again. This time, and with his help, several core insights emerged. First, the specific set of behaviors I displayed is *not* who I am. The facilitative behaviors are just that, behaviors, some among many possible responses in any given set of circumstances. I could and can behave otherwise.

I realized that even though my intention is usually up front for me as I act, it is not the only thing that matters. In a given interaction, there is both my intention and the effect of my actions on the listener. If I'm aware and sensitive, I may be able to adjust my words, facial expression or tone, in the moment if or when I sense discomfort or distress in the other. Many times, though, I'm so focused on my own experience that I pay little or no attention to what's happening for the other person as I speak. When I plow ahead this way, and the other is not on the same page, it can be very damaging to the quality of the interaction.

What I also discovered from the stormy interaction with

Jessica was that my intentions were not hundred percent pure, as I would have liked to believe. Of the insights so far, this was most humbling, because it flew in the face of my belief in my own innocence. When I looked closely, I discovered that deep down, I had a certain desire to control the situation, maybe even to recap Jessica's experience and move on. But, I still reassured myself, thinking 'mostly I was just wanting to be helpful, really I was. I didn't know it would be a problem.' And this was true.

After about an additional hour of work, tears and confusion, heart-wrenching and unstinting honesty, with continuing patience and some effective summarizing on my husband's part, I finally was able to fall asleep—humbled and wiser—intending to call Jessica the next day to clear the air.

When we spoke the next morning, Jessica was unforgiving. "I don't give a rat's ass what your intentions were," she said, and added that what I had done was not only unhelpful, it had been woefully inappropriate and particularly galling to her. She specifically said, "The road to hell is paved with good intentions." While I had heard that proverb many times before, never had it penetrated so deeply. It is indeed hell for me not to be able to clean things up, to clarify a misunderstanding and restore harmony. But this didn't happen that morning, nor after another conversation I had with Jessica in a second, and final, attempt to patch things up.

What I did learn from these challenging, painful, but illuminating interactions is that I do not need to be facilitating to be authentically myself. I also noticed my deep-seated tendency to make myself look good, asserting a positive intent when in fact there was a bit of mud in the mixture. And I began to grasp that, as much as I might hope that my good intentions will carry the day, they might not: the effect my actions have on another person might not necessarily be congruent with my intent.

In the end, with Jessica, I had to 'leave bad enough alone.' All my efforts to make amends, to take responsibility for my behavior and to listen to her were of no avail. She was not willing to come to any mutual understanding or forgiveness, at least not together with me. Helping me realize that sometimes the best I can do is to 'leave bad enough alone' was Jessica's parting gift and lesson for me. Jessica was the perfect teacher, providing a profound lesson at an ideal time, and I am grateful, (really I am!) for the deep learning she facilitated in me.

There have been numerous times since when my well intended actions or words have offended the other, and I have often attempted to modify my behavior to repair the damage or prevent something similar from happening in the future. I have learned much about body language. (A simple hand gesture can turn an otherwise innocuous remark into a perceived insult.) I have realized the importance of tone of voice and pacing. (Slow and calm is usually better, and both are a challenge for me at times!) I have noticed a persistent tendency to deceive myself, make myself look more virtuous or well-meaning than I really am. I have experienced serious negative fallout when the way I have asserted my positive intentions inadvertently but perceptibly left the other person feeling in the one-down position.

Here's a specific example: John, a sharp academic acquaintance of mine, said to me during a tangle we had over the holidays, "Jill, when you say 'you're just trying to clear things up, you simply want to find out what really happened,' how do you think that makes *me* feel? As though I'm *not* doing that… as though I'm *not* wanting to know the truth? It puts me at the bottom of an interlocutory mudslide. It bugs me, and I find it intellectually and personally insulting." After that exchange, I was speechless for a while! Yet, this interaction was the beginning of a profound change and new phase of personal growth for me.

Dealing with Jessica, I accepted the maxim 'The road to hell is paved with good intentions,' quite literally. I set about trying to 'improve myself,' to anticipate the response of the other, to gather feedback regarding the effect my words and actions were having on others, and to change myself for the better. This has not been in vain.

At the same time, since last year's holidays, my understanding of the truths in these situations is now both clearer and subtler:

- I have come to realize that no matter how hard I work, and even at my most present and authentic moments, I can not always manage to say or do things in a way that works for everyone in the way I hope or intend that it will.
- When, as inevitably happens on occasion, I am misunderstood and/or my good intentions have confused or upset someone, as happened with my relative, I take it less personally.
- I try not to avoid my share of responsibility for the tangle, but the way I am seen by others is less important than what I know to be true for myself. I rely less on others to know and be myself.
- I have begun to be more accepting of the occasional, but inevitable discomfort in interpersonal interactions – and I have (at better times!), a certain healthy detachment from the outcomes.

These shifts to increasingly deeper levels of understanding have, on the one hand, been gradual and incremental. Yet with this recent and precipitous jump forward, it feels like the work of many years past has somehow been integrated more deeply. I love it when this happens!

My ongoing work is still to be to be as clear and respectful as I possibly can. That hasn't changed. The new dimensions I am now experiencing are greater trust and gentleness toward myself. At times I am in touch with a spaciousness and tender strength, even when there has been an upset or difference of opinion. I can experience the clear and quiet calm that comes from the acceptance of ambiguities and misunderstanding. It feels like a page in my life history has turned, and I've begun a new chapter.

Related reading:

Almaas, A. H. (2002). *Spacecruiser Inquiry: True guidance for the inner journey*. Boston: Shambhala

Ruiz, Don Miguel (1997). *The Four Agreements: A practical guide to personal freedom. A Toltec wisdom book.* San Rafael, CA: Amber-Allen Publishing

Tannen, Deborah (1986). *That's Not What I Meant: How conversational style makes or breaks relationships.* NY: Ballantine Books

Thich Nhat Hanh (2001). *Anger: Wisdom for cooling the flames.* Berkeley, Parallax Press

Reflections: *Recall an experience where it felt like you were on the 'road to hell' because of a misunderstanding? How did it feel in your body? Then consider a situation where your best intentions were at odds with what happened for the other person? How did you become aware of this and how did you deal with the discrepancy?*

"I now understand that my welfare is only possible if I acknowledge my unity with all the people of the world without exception." Leo Tolstoy

"Humankind has not woven the web of life. We are but one thread within it. Whatever we do to the web, we do to ourselves." Chief Seattle

ᕼᓭᕼ

No One Hits First

…in a conflict situation. Ask around. Everyone is quite convinced that it was the other person who 'started it.' I recall the sting of anger and dismay I've felt in my viscera when my husband (or daughter, friend, or colleague) said something that seemed cutting or abrupt to me. I feel hurt, hard done by, jerked around, ignored… fill in the blank. And so do they. The point is that in conflict situations, when emotions are negative and strong, most of us only think about ourselves.

In most conflict situations (perhaps in all of them), when verbal attacks ensue, they arise inside out of a basic instinct for self-defense. I first heard this radical notion in a basic conflict resolution course two decades ago. Hmmm, I thought. Could it really be that people only behave in an aggressive, hurtful manner if they themselves are feeling attacked or threatened?

I have come to believe it is true. So simple, the insight, yet radical and transformative when we can remember it in the pinch and clinch of differences.

Here's an example, one of many. I was working with Sarah; we had developed and just finished the first day of a communication workshop. We were debriefing the day. Sarah said, "You really didn't do a very good job handling the paraphrasing exercise this morning, Jill. I think you were disrespectful of some of the students. " Feeling ambushed, I retorted, "Well, you got rather defensive when Joe said he was confused about your instructions." And to my initial counterattack I added, "It was good your boss didn't see that."

Adding to the irony and poignancy of this situation is that we were both reasonably skilled professionals, yet didn't manage to do any better than this.

So where does 'no one hits first' come in and how would it have made a difference here?

After the two first interactions we were both feeling attacked. Sarah said I hadn't done a good job. I felt stung, 'hit first.' Without thinking, my first reaction was to lash out and hit back. It was only in the untangling process that I was able to step out of my reactive mode and become curious about what was motivating Sarah when she 'criticized' me. As I asked what she was thinking when she said I hadn't done a good job, she shared that she had understood we would be handling that part of the process together, and I had just jumped in and taken in over. So she was stinging from having been ignored, felt dismissed and not sure she could trust me.

Sarah ultimately also managed to shift gears and get curious. But bear with me while I back up a little to shed more light on the process. 'Shifting gears' is much easier said than done. What does it actually mean, and how can and does it happen? When I am in conflict or a misunderstanding, I have a very narrow focus (almost entirely on myself), and I am usually driving on automatic: past patterns and assumptions about the world and other people are in my driver's seat. If somehow I can start to see a larger picture—that I'm driving my car, in a habitual reactive way, and that the other, in this case, Sarah, is *also* driving her car, and we're bumping in to each other—then I have stepped back, and have a better chance of seeing that there could be another perspective involved. This is a start, perhaps a prerequisite to shifting gears: stepping back to see there's another point of view.

Becoming: Journeying toward Authenticity

In the heat of the clash this is excruciatingly hard to do. The motivation in my case comes from two places: first I have the experience of many past crashes, collisions and wrecks and know how painful and damaging they are. Remembering this in the heat of the moment enables me to step back. Secondly, I have experiences of when I have actually managed to 'shift gears' and things have resolved without, or with less, crashing and emotional damage. The awareness both of the better and the worse outcomes serve as motivators. I now have a choice.

But then I have to have some other gears into which I can shift. I need some other communication and collaboration skills. Else I am stuck. And these skills are exactly what Sarah and I had been teaching! And they're available in many courses and books these days.

When, in the untangling, she explored what had happened for me, we both learned (for I wasn't even really aware of it at the time) that I was feeling particularly sensitive and insulted because I had thought the debrief of the exercise had gone very well. Furthermore I prided myself on dealing respectfully with students, and finally, had completely forgotten we'd agreed to handle that part of the material together. That's another generative effect of the process: we often discover new things about ourselves, the other person, or the dynamic between us.

If either one of us had remembered 'no one hits first,' we could have stopped the conflagration before it had begun to rage so hotly. We could have avoided the destructive flare-up, clarified assumptions, learned more about each other and ourselves.

For example, when a close friend said, abruptly, "No, I don't want help setting up the storage space," I swallowed my initial irritation, and my own sense of feeling hit. (After all, I had simply offered to help!) I managed not to say anything sharp, and noticed, oh, maybe he's feeling hit. Wonder why? When I described what I noticed and asked him what was up, it turned out I seemed to be his big brother again, always offering a better way to do something.

Even if both people are aware of the principle, it is nevertheless challenging to catch it in the moment and head off the conflict or hard feelings. But the beauty and power of the insight is that it only takes one person to recognize the dynamic and step out of it. Either person can break the lock step.

In the situation above it would also have interrupted the reactive cycle if my friend had noticed he was 'feeling hit' and explained in more detail how my request was affecting him without my having asked. In contrast to dancing the tango, it only takes one person to recognize that someone's feeling hit. That's good news.

I'm not suggesting that this is easy—to remember in the heat of a challenging situation to recall that no one hits first. And then to figure out in a mutually collaborative manner what's really going on.

But it is possible! And deeply healing and beneficial when we can manage it. It's even exciting, creative and almost magical. It takes self awareness, being in the moment, willing to shift from judgment and defensiveness to curiosity. You also have to remember to breathe!

Related reading:

Chodron, Thubten (2001). *Working with Anger.* Ithaca: Snow Lion Press
Harper, Gary (2004). *The Joy of Conflict Resolution: Transforming victims, villains and heroes in the workplace and at home.* Gabriola Island, BC: New Society Publishers
Rosenberg, Marshall (1999). *Nonviolent Communication: A language of compassion.* Encinitas, CA: PuddleDancer Press
Thich Nhat Hanh ((2005). *Being Peace.* Berkeley: Parallax Press

Reflections: *Recall a difficult situation in which you felt 'hit first,' maybe out of the blue. How did you respond? Imagine yourself getting curious instead of feeling hurt? If you were able to do this, what might you say, feel do? In your imagination, how would this scenario turn out compared to the 'real' one? When you have a challenging situation ahead of you, consider role-playing with a friend to practice. Discuss the experience with your friend, noticing what worked, what didn't, and what you'd like to take into the actual situation.*

Becoming: Journeying toward Authenticity

"Forget not that the earth likes to feel your bare feet and the winds long to play with your hair." Kahlil Gibran

"We do not cease to play because we grow old: we grow old because we cease to play." George Bernard Shaw

Work and/or Play?

Early in my first marriage to Wolf, the Austrian mountain climber I had met on an international exchange program, I bumped up against one of my belief systems: Work is work, and play is play, and they are not supposed to be mixed. Wolf, from the beginning of our relationship, had a knack for combining work and play. This was something I didn't know how to do, didn't want to at first. Learning to see the connections and interplay between the two was a painful, but rewarding, life lesson.

I remember one particular incident. We were on a field trip to Salzburg with a group of students, and there was a big agenda: camp had to be set up, jobs assigned so the work would flow well, data gathered, presentations planned. I was in my usual mode, inclined to tackle the project with efficiency, organization, and focus. This came quite easily to me. I had, after all, been deeply steeped in the Protestant work ethic. Hard work brought good rewards. At least this is what I had picked up along the way and believed sincerely, almost religiously. Hard work benefited both individuals and society, and working diligently was nothing short of an obligation. Doubtless.

Part way to our destination, Wolf radioed ahead to the drivers in the auto caravan saying "Everyone pull over as soon as you can." We all came to a halt near a mountain lake bordered by a small village, and piled out to hear, "Let's have a picnic. It's too nice to just drive straight on." This had not been planned and it was not clear how the picnic would take shape.

The sun was shining, glinting light diamonds off the deep blue green of the lake. The grass was soft to sit on, like a pillow cushion, emerald green with summer luxuriance. The meadow near the lake seemed to be inviting us to linger awhile. There was a lot of laughter, good humor and some chaos as we muddled through figuring out what food we had, or needed to buy, to feed us all. It turned out splendidly: the dark and savory Austrian bread, an assortment of local cheeses and sausages filled our senses and our stomachs; and according to good Austrian practice, there was even some chilled beer swilled. Even with all this pleasure, we would probably be on our way again in an hour or so. You could actually feel people's spirits lift. Everyone had a good time. Except me.

I was grouchy, and somehow confused. We had a mission, there were jobs to be done. This stop would make us late, and besides, we were supposed to be working. That was what this trip was about. Having fun along the way felt like a contamination. I also didn't like the feeling of being left out when all the others were enjoying themselves. Yet the isolation did not crack my belief system at the time: It was work *or* play, and not work *and* play. Much time would pass until I loosened up!

Years later, living in Germany, and with two young children, I applied for and was accepted into a masters program in England for Biometry—the technical word for statistics for the natural sciences. I had been accepted because of my practical experience, but I was in well over my depth as far as the math and statistics were concerned. I woke up many nights in a cold sweat and worked like a dog, but still didn't pass the first semester's exams at the Masters level. I ended up having to be examined on that material all over again the following year, along with taking the exams for the second semester's work.

In the end I passed them all with flying colors. But hard work it was. I remember staying up nights learning matrix multiplication and the analysis of variance for complex experimental designs. It was no picnic! Literally, as well as figuratively, I sometimes got cold feet, as well as hands, studying until the wee small hours in the garage room where I was staying, and I often sat on the vanity dangling my feet in the sink to warm them up. It was as though all my blood was needed in my brain to meet the academic demands, none left for hands or feet.

Wolf was supportive of my education. Everyone had pitched in, my kids, family, neighbors and friends, to make it possible. When Wolf was telling a colleague about my time in England, he emphasized what fun I was having—saying that people on his team didn't do anything that wasn't fun too. I felt diminished and insulted. What did he know! How hard I was working! Fun? That wasn't part of it. I was doing a job, and it was a hard, challenging one at that.

But in spite of the artificial separation of work and play in my mind, in reality there were not only plenty of good times mixed with the hard study, there were rich personal experiences that opened my heart and expanded my horizons. At the university I had made some good friends among the students, many of whom were much younger than I. We played some rousing squash games, and they included me in local holidays since I was away from family. I stayed in touch with several of them for years.

I also remember a weekend excursion to Yorkshire to help harvest grapes on a small private vineyard, where I enjoyed some of the best food I've ever eaten. The woman of the house cooked feasts while we picked. Scrumptious, rich and bubbling meat pies with thick, flaky pastry; scones that melted in your mouth served with homemade preserves. It was like being at a five star hotel, except we were working for our room and board!

I took trips into London, to the British Museum and the theater district, and had great fun helping organize an end of semester bash for all the stats students. Oh, and I almost forgot about the pub crawls with Ian and Graham! But despite these rewarding and stimulating times, for me, these months were first and foremost about hard work.

I didn't grasp the wisdom and the pleasure of the mixture: I still didn't have room in my psyche for work *and* play. It was work, work, and more work. Even though I had played along the way, I didn't get the beauty and richness of allowing them to co-exist.

I'm not sure when that changed—it's been a slow but steady process in which I have gradually moved out of the usual mode of work *or* play, and even that of work *and* play. There were occasions where I experienced work *as* play and play *as* work and the possibility of the overlap or interplay of the two. The distinctions began to blur altogether.

When I am 'playing' tennis, I am actually 'working' very hard, to keep my eye on the ball, to stay light on my feet, to anticipate the path of the ball and get my racket ready. It's so easy to give in to my habitual sloppiness and let my eye drift to where my opponent is standing, or to worry about the score, or what will happen if I lose this point, or maybe even to think about my grocery list! What's critical in the moment is to watch the ball straight to its contact with the racquet if the stroke is to be sound. And that takes serious concentration. Playing well can be hard work! When I manage to play points this way, the result is intensely satisfying. I come alive, I'm paying full attention, am calling on many skills, feeling the richness of the challenge. The co-mingling of work and play is very juicy!

It works the other way around, too. I've noticed that when I sit down to write, if I slip into the feeling I'm supposed to be 'working,' I can experience a kind of heaviness, the time drags, the blank page stares back at me in a kind of showdown. When I come to my writing with a lightness, a curiosity and playfulness about what will flow from inside me onto the paper, it feels like my creativity is engaged, there's a newness, a trust in the process, and the words often pour out easily. There is ample empirical research to support this idea. When we bring play or humor into a work-sphere, productivity climbs, sales soar, and absenteeism drops. People feel better about themselves, their work and their lives in general.

Play can even be powerful in what many would not consider a laughing matter: spirituality. I experienced a radical shift in myself on an occasion where I brought lightness and play into my spiritual practice. I was attending a spiritual retreat where the particular teaching focused on living well and authentically. One particular talk was about how lightness and even play can bring a new perspective to our spiritual work and personal development. During an exercise with another student I had a break-though experience where my old and structured self essentially 'popped' like a balloon. It, and I, were simply no longer there in the usual way. It was unanticipated and startling. I was just sitting there, present, light and clear, no separations, judgments or shoulds. Just aliveness, ease and freshness.

With lightness and curiosity, my familiar experience of separateness—me and you, right and wrong, work and play— gave way to clarity, and even a glimpse of the interconnectedness and interdependence of all life.

Related reading:
Edwards, Betty ((1989). *Drawing on the Right Side of the Brain: A course in enhancing creativity and artistic confidence.* NY: G. P. Putnam's Sons
Fulghum, Robert (2003). *All I Really Need to Know I Learned in Kindergarten.* NY: Random House
Kingsolver, Barbara (2007). *Animal Vegetable, Miracle: A year of food life.* NY: HarperCollins

Reflections: *What do your values, patterns, and ethics have to say regarding the value of work? Play? Mixing the two? How do you combine them, or not, in your life? What other areas of your life do you keep separate that might be energized, synergized, if combined?*

*"We don't think ourselves into a new way of acting, we
act ourselves into a new way of thinking."*
Larry Bossidy and Ram Charan

"You can't stop the waves, but you can learn to surf." *Jack Kornfield*

~ᔐᐯᔐ~

Fake It 'til You Make It

This whole book and all the essays in it are supposedly about authenticity, becoming more real, in touch with yourself, true and whole. So what the heck can an idea like faking it, in any way shape or form whatsoever, have to do with it? Get me outta here! This is starting to sound like a sham.

But wait, hold on. There are times when the kind of faking it to which I'm referring can actually help us along the journey.

When I first heard the phrase 'fake it 'til you make it' I smiled. Somewhere inside I related to the notion of faking it. It is something we all do occasionally, kids, parents, politicians, teachers… Almost all of us prevaricate, tell half truths, engage at times in white lies of some sort of other. And there's that especially egregious version of faking it: rationalizing what we're doing by making it look good, swelling ourselves into righteousness. 'Oh, honey, I'm not nagging. I really just have your best interests in mind.'

These behaviors are not something I defend, but there's something normal, human about them, and I suggest that acknowledging and accepting our imperfections and the lack of genuineness is more likely to lead to change than rejection and condemnation. But if these essays are primarily about authenticity, and reaching for those aspects of ourselves that may be finer, deeper, more wholesome, you may ask again, 'What does an essay on faking it contribute?'

For one, faking it can help us over challenging humps, give us a bootstrap when we need it badly. I have a friend who was starting her own business, from nothing. Ground up. Instead of putting the whole truth out, elaborating about the cautious and unsure beginnings, she took on the feelings and the language of having arrived, having a functioning and well-established enterprise with several people working for her. And before long, that's exactly what had happened. Good for her.

Yet the version of faking it which I'd like to explore is of a different nature still. There is a way in which we can take the high road on the outside even if we are uncertain of whether we even know where, or how, to find the high road on the inside. There is a Zen saying that says 'assume the posture of enlightenment, and you are already there.' What I'm referring here to when I say 'faking it' is along those lines.

Consider one of the many situations in which my first response is not particularly collaborative: I might be feeling defensive or actually aggressive, or some combination of the above. If I nevertheless manage to speak respectfully, this 'trick' actually transforms, or at least shifts and reorients, my inner landscape. Here's a specific example. My partner has not done what we'd agreed to (or what I thought we'd agreed to), in the way of sharing household responsibilities. What I'm feeling at the time is blame, like I'm being taken advantage of, and grumpy. If I were 'honest' and true to those feelings in the moment, I might say something like 'That's really unfair, you never do your part, you're selfish and thoughtless and treat me like a pile of dirt.' Long pause. What good is that kind of authenticity? Not much.

But if I 'fake it,' and take the higher road, (even though it contradicts my momentary feelings), and speak assertively I could say something like 'When I find dishes in the sink after work and it's your day for clean up, I feel frustrated. I'd really like it if we share the kitchen jobs as we'd agreed.' What's interesting is that I *actually* feel different inside when I do that. No longer so put upon or at the effect of the other person's actions.

And there's benefit even if the person doesn't apologize, jump up, and run into the kitchen. It's about me, and how I'm relating to the situation and to myself. I've spoken clearly about my views and preferences in a way that's respectful of everyone involved.

We've talked now some about faking it. But what might 'make it' mean? That's something for each of us to decide in the moment and in our lives, maybe even each day anew. 'Making it' on one day might mean I manage not to shout at my kids or husband. On another day it might mean I allocate my time so that there space for meditation and quiet and that I sense my arms and legs while I do the dishes, or don't binge on sweets. Or that I don't give in to the feelings of worthlessness and laziness, or that just because I've had one piece of chocolate I don't give in and eat the whole bar. Or that I create a nourishing meal when it seemed like there was nothing in the fridge or cupboard. Or contribute to something that will make a difference to others. Each day, each one of us will need to decide, in an ongoing way, if and how 'faking it' might be useful.

Remember the movie The King and I? There was a song that went, "*Whenever I feel afraid, I hold my head erect and whistle a happy tune …And the result of this deception is very strange to tell, Whenever I fool the people I fear, I fool myself as well.*"

The point of 'faking it til you make it' is along these lines. But more than just fooling ourselves, often it happens that there is an unmistakable shift inside, toward the kind of authenticity that is respectful of ourselves and of the other person as well. And if it doesn't happen at first, or completely, keep faking it! We are a combination of our inner worlds and our outer worlds and they are interconnected but there are time lags. When we feel crappy inside, it's awfully easy to do a lot of damage to ourselves, our relationships. And we menace our communities and the planet as well when we act out our impulses of greed, bitterness, or from a momentary, or habitual, sense of inadequacy.

If we manage to make these shifts, it not only overrides our petty self-focus, it can actually change the way we feel, so that later, next time, the lag might not be so great.

I think you get it that I'm not suggesting 'faking it' in any but respectful and constructive ways. Nor am I proposing that we be deceptive or false in any lasting manner. It's a tool, skillful means, as they say in spiritual circles, to move toward that to which we aspire—authenticity, clarity for ourselves, congruence with our higher self and our ideals. So when I 'fool' the people out there, for example, by speaking assertively when I feel like blaming and whining, I can gradually shift the feelings and attitudes inside. I can create a positive experience of responding constructively even when I feel cantankerous, and find that the more appropriately I act, the less ill tempered I feel.

And if it all breaks down, of course I can go have a stiff drink, pound a pillow, call a friend or write in my journal: whinge, cry, shout, scream, own that I am feeling distraught and completely a mess. And I don't even try to fake myself out of this. (Just kidding about the stiff drink.) Writing at such times, instead of whining or blaming, is a kind of authenticity that can be cathartic and maybe help us get a different perspective too.

Sometimes I feel like the world is falling apart, that there is nothing healthy in us humans, that we all, and especially our leaders, are a bunch of fear-driven, hateful, ignorant morons. Were I to act from this place it would either be out of despair, hate and probably hopelessness, which is not going to bear much fruit. Or I might give up and just say there's nothing I can do about it anyway, so just carry on with the old, selfish ways. This can lead to the so-called tragedy of the commons that Garrett Hardin elucidated.

If, however, in the face of feeling and perceiving disintegration, I act generatively—connect, cooperate, help my neighbor, perpetrate random acts of kindness—I am actually transformed. I have not so much fooled, as reoriented myself. I begin to notice all the kindness, the generosity, the inner and outer synchronicity and wholeness that exist in the world as surely as do greed and ignorance.

We can choose how we act by paying attention to what we want rather than what we don't want. Sometimes I can almost feel the sub-atomic particles reorienting as I shift my language, my posture, my behavior. Each day we open our eyes and there's a dawning. Each moment of each day we have choices. Inner and outer. When our inner inclinations threaten to take us down, dampen and drudge us, one option is to look the other direction, and 'fake it.'

Related reading:

Almaas, A. H. (1986). *Essence: The Diamond Approach to inner realization.* York Beach, ME: Samuel Weiser, Inc.

Hardin, Garrett (1968). *The Tragedy of the Commons.* Science: 162(1968):1243-1248

Jeffers, Susan (1987). *Feel the Fear and Do It Anyway.* NY: Ballantine Books

Sandburg, Carl ((1922). *Rootabaga Stories.* NY: Harcourt Brace & Co.

Reflections: *Think of a situation where you were scrupulously honest and wished you hadn't been? How might you have been able to 'fake it' in a constructive way, if at all? Recall a situation where you actually know you were behaving in a fake way. What was the outcome? How is this different from 'faking it' until you 'make it'? Think of a typical challenging day in your life and explore what 'making it' might mean.*

"I know what the great cure is: it is to give up, to relinquish, to surrender, so that our little hearts may beat in unison with the great heart of the world." Henry Miller

"Believe there is a great power silently working all things for good, behave yourself and never mind the rest." Beatrix Potter

Control and Surrender

Related reading:
Almaas, A. H. (1988). *The Pearl beyond Price: Integration of personality into Being: An object relations approach.* Berkeley: Diamond Books
Barks, Coleman (1995). *The Essential Rumi.* NY: HarperCollins
Huxley, Aldous (2004). *The Perennial Pholosophy: An interpretation of the great mystics, east and west.* NY: Perennial Classics, HarperCollins
Schucman, Helen and William Thetford (1985). A *Course in Miracles.* Tiburon, CA: Foundation for Inner Peace
Tolle, Eckhart (1999). *The Power of Now.* Vancouver, BC: Namaste Publishing

*"If you obey all the rules you miss all
the fun."* Katharine Hepburn

*"Joint undertakings stand a better chance when they
benefit both sides."* Euripides

Where There's a Will, There's a Way

….she was told. And she also was urged to 'never take no for an answer.' My mother was a Leo, tall, strong, sometimes bold. Maybe she acted boldly at times in part because she'd heard these phrases again and again in the course of her growing up. They seem to have soaked deeply into her psyche, and they did, in turn, into mine as well. She'd absorbed them from her dad and I had absorbed them from her. They were part of my philosophy of life for many years.

There's a determination in the words. When I say them to myself and listen with my inner ear, I feel full, red, alive with capacity and creativity, ready to take on whatever challenges might come my way. Long ago, I saw an ad on TV promoting a courier service. The video clip emphasized that when things go smoothly and everything is running as scheduled, there's no particular 'juice' to the job. It's when difficulties or roadblocks arise that things get spicy and people must get creative, explore alternatives, find different modalities, shift into different gears. The team and this company would always (that's what the ad would have had us believe), find a way to deliver the goods!

I remember the excitement I felt, my hair standing on end. It was dark outside and I was by myself in the living room. The children were in bed, my husband was away. I was inspired by

Becoming: Journeying toward Authenticity

the ad's images of success and the feeling of accomplishment in the face of odds. I think the film clip spoke to me so strongly because the philosophy had been laid down in an early groove in my psyche: a commitment to making things work, finding a way. The enthusiasm and positive energy of the people in the courier company resonated with my sense of myself at the time and how I wanted to be.

One day I had a chance to put this into practice. I was on the bus on my way to the airport to fly to Belize for a four-week stint as a volunteer diver with Coral Cay Conservation, an organization that works to protect endangered coral reefs. Half way there I looked at my ticket and realized I was supposed to have flown the day before! My face went white, my heart started to pound. But it wasn't long before I began to think, 'OK. What do I do now?' I began plotting strategies, considering alternatives, weighing best and worst-case scenarios, prioritizing the things that needed to be done.

It was a hair-raising experience, but the upshot is that I made it. My mother's counsel echoed from the corners of my memory and it was her advice that got me there. Or was it? It also took the cooperation of people working for Air Canada and those with a small Mexican airline, who let me take my seat a day late, rather than canceling the ticket, not to mention the goodwill and flexibility of the staff at Coral Cay, who had had to make an extra run with the fuel boat so I could join up with the other volunteers.

It was a kind of high, skimming over the water, in the moist, fragrant warm air, frigate birds and black pelicans circling overhead, palm trees seemingly waving a welcome. I learned from the volunteers that the first night they'd spent had been in a dingy, skuzzy hotel, and I had finessed this unsavory experience by being a day late. They said I should count myself lucky to have missed it!

Even so, I began to feel not only the thrill of the successful trip, the satisfaction of having arrived in good time, but I also began to sense the price my actions extracted. When I'm in the throes of an adventure, such as the trip to Belize, it's hard to notice the larger perspective. I really thrive on the challenge and the uncertainty, and love believing I am 'making things work.' I can become quite oblivious to the inconvenience, even troubles or discomfort, that I might be causing others in my way. But I'm beginning to learn.

I'm finding there are costs on several levels to exerting my will to find a way. What may work very well for me, growing out of my familiar and comfortable 'never take no' mode, may well come across to others as pushy—insensitive at best, and sometimes even downright inconsiderate or manipulative.

My husband and I were sharing a Christmas holiday with four of the children of our blended family at a cabin in the evergreen woods of Vancouver Island. It was early in our second marriage and the first holiday season with our grown children. We were all getting along quite well, each feeling a little awkward and new in the situation, but being sensitive to each other and the common space. We had gone out in the softly falling snow to find and cut our own Christmas tree. We were feeling the peace of the season and the deep quiet of the cedar trees surrounding us. After finding a perfect tree, we returned to the cabin to enjoy the cracking fire and the cracked crab we had gotten for Christmas eve.

When conversation turned to the possibility of skiing, I got it in my head it would be fun for the kids to ski together. It was a perfect example of not taking no for an answer. Despite obvious lack of interest on the part of the grown children, I persisted for some time, suggesting options, trying to arrange transportation, calling various ski slopes. It was clear to everyone but me that there had been enough togetherness, and the kids were ready to do things on their own. The fallout of that interaction created some ill-will and discomfort that lasted for years. Had they all wanted to go skiing, my assertiveness and creativity might have helped find a way. What created the tension was my pushing my personal agenda so hard, my inability to be sensitive to the 'no' hanging palpably in the air. It was extremely painful for me when I realized what had happened and the damage that had been done.

At a deeper level, I believe that just as we are not the directors of the dance, we are not really 'making it happen.' Events are flowing along, we can be aligned and in tune, or we can be out of joint and at cross purposes. There are times when our well-intended efforts and pushing just tangles things up, creates distress and pain for ourselves as well as others. And sometimes, no amount of will can create a way anyway!

So when does it make sense to 'go for it' and work hard for something or someone, and when is it appropriate to back off, be quiet and let things happen? How can we assess what degree of assertiveness or coming forward is appropriate in different situations? In my experience, there's no 'one size fits all' answer to these challenging questions.

For me, the larger learning is that being deeply attached to any particular outcome invites suffering. Yet within that context, we might still want to reflect on when and how to come forward, and also develop the sensitivity about when and how to back off. And the trickiest bit may be acquiring the wisdom to tell the difference!

For some of us speaking out and standing up for ourselves is easy, and slowing down, listening, taking others into account are challenges. For others, listening—being attuned, doing all we can to see that others' needs are met—comes easily. Sometimes we have a hard time even knowing what we want, let alone taking steps to put our needs or interests forward. Some of us might find it hard to believe that we have a right to be heard, let alone sticking with it to see that our needs are met, or at least acknowledged.

Ideally we can develop all three skills: coming forward, deferring or waiting, and delicately sensing which is appropriate in a given situation, blending and intertwining them as in a multihued tapestry or lively dance.

Related reading:
Linnae, Ann ((1999). *Deep Water Passage: A spiritual journey at midlife.*
Boston: Simon & Schuster
Mauer, Robert (2004). *One Small Step Can Change Your Life.* NY:
Workman Publishing
Ruiz, Don Miguel (1997). *The Four Agreements: A practical guide to
personal freedom, A Toltec wisdom book.* San Rafael, CA: Amber-Allen
Publishing

Reflections: *What's your challenge: coming forward, backing off, or
learning to tell the difference? What is a situation where you blasted ahead
and later came to see that you had been less than effective? What, if anything,
might have helped you assess the situation more accurately? When did you
not speak up when you wish you had? How could you equip yourself to
respond more assertively next time?*

*"Right now a moment of time is passing by!
We must become that moment." Paul Cezanne*

"Ah! What a day-to-day affair life is." Jules Laforgue

∿ᏉᏟᏉ

Use It or Lose It!

I heard the phrase for the first time about twenty years ago. I've been intrigued ever since. It's compact, somehow intuitive, exhortative.

"Is your sex life deflating into middle age? Maybe you need to 'use it or lose it!'"

"New Alzheimer's Research concludes that when it comes to memory, there might just be something to the old adage 'use it or lose it.'"

"Despite government efforts to make us aware of the health benefits of exercise, the number of Canadians sufficiently active to remain healthy has stayed the same for over five years—at roughly 37 percent." (From a 'Use It or Lose It' Quiz.)

These are just a few of the results I got when I googled 'use it or lose it.'

What does the maxim really mean, and what flavor does it add to my life?

When I hear the phrase I can feel two possibilities. One is inspirational, one is ominous. The exclamation mark that usually follows the phrase sometimes makes it feel like a threat. 'You better use it, by golly, or you're gonna lose it!' There is a menacing quality to the words. Sex, health, brainpower. Body, mind, maybe even spirit. Will all these atrophy if I ignore them? That's what it can sound like when I listen to the message of voice number one.

And I respond 'Oh dear! Oh my! That would be terrible, It's all downhill; I'll run out of steam; the muscles, of my body, my mind and my heart will deteriorate and I'll be a big mess!' Inadvertently my heart starts to beat a bit faster, and life seems like a race that I might be losing, or at the very least, falling behind... There's a giant critic in the sky looking down on me, saying 'Get cracking or else!'

Now, in some cases, fear can indeed be a motivator. The fear of radical, disastrous climate change might help us modify our consumer lifestyle patterns. The fear of dying prematurely of lung cancer might encourage one to stop smoking. However, my experience is that when I act out of fear, feeling pressured by a fear-based inner critic, I soon get resentful, and/or feel self-pity and am likely to quit soon—whether it be doing the lat pull downs, avoiding sweets in my diet, keeping up with my spiritual practices, or taking positive action for the planet. Fear is a slave driver, and I haven't had good experiences with slave drivers!

Flashback to the personal growth workshop in Germany where each person in turn sat in the center of the circle and received people's feedback. The participants shared their impressions of the person in the 'hot seat.' When it was my turn to be in the center, people commented on my personal power, attentiveness, focus, warmth... I had some difficulty allowing it all to soak in, but I managed! Then one person presented a different picture: 'You seem like a slave driver, Jill. You're so hard on yourself, and I'd be afraid you'd be that way with me too.' The person may have said 'task-master' but I heard 'slave driver.'

Whichever word it actually was, I've never forgotten the sting as the words sank in. Inside I said 'Me? A task master, a slave driver? Why, I'm just efficient, like getting things done. Sure I can be task focused but I ...' and I started making excuses for myself, trying to counteract the effect of the message. And it's true, the slave driver was only one part of me. But the flavor of the first voice saying 'use it or lose' it is just that slave driver, an introjected critical persona that has a self-image of me as too fat, too lazy, never doing enough, not measuring up.

One way I've learned to deal with the inner critic response is to tell it to simply "F--k off, get off my back!" I might also counter its message with something like "I've been working for years to get out from under just these kinds of voices and at this stage in life, I just don't need your services anymore. I just got my Canadian health care system Gold Card and am a died-in-the-wool, no-longer-able-or-wanting-to-deny-it, ready-to-accept-all-the-privileges-that-come-my-way, Senior! and I really don't need critical voices breathing down my neck, so just move it out!"

Hey, it feels great to say that!

I definitely don't need the inner critic, and I'm so glad I finally have some effective strategies for dealing with it.

And if that were all there were to the implications of the phrase 'use it or lose it,' I'd like to think that after all the years of cognitive therapy and personal work I've done, I would have managed to banish the slave driver, and I'd not pay any attention to the 'You'd better, or else' voice.

But there's more. There is another implication of the words 'use if or lose it.' It can be inspirational—genuinely motivating, even empowering. To me it says something like 'If you use it, you're less likely to lose it.' Or 'Even if you do ultimately have to lose it (in the end we're all gonna die), if you use it along the way, you'll more likely have the pleasure of enjoying it for much longer. Go for it!'

Go for it! Now there's something that appeals to me, have fun, live it up, all the while embracing paradox and mystery. While I am not in charge of life, or of the way that it unfolds and changes, I am part of this flow. I do not control it, yet there *are* areas where my personal choices have implications and consequences. Every day I can make choices that contribute to keeping fit and staying functional.

The emotional, spiritual and cognitive realms also respond to ongoing choices to use or lose them: cultivating friendships, being aware and living in the moment—such capacities too are in the 'use them or lose them' category.

Some concrete examples. I've starting doing Sudoku number puzzles. And I'm getting a lot of pleasure out of 'using' my number skills this way. I quite look forward to my daily dose of numbers in this particular, challenging way, pushing the edges by tackling the 'Super Difficult Puzzles.' Or memory: of course I forget things, but I manage to find most of the stuff I search for in the far corners of my mind, usually fairly quickly. Not always of course. Sometimes my husband will say something like 'What was the name of that book Paul mentioned?' and I will know immediately that I haven't the foggiest idea. The information just didn't get stored at all. I'll know right away that I don't know. Which has its own sort of satisfaction. But then he might ask, "Who was it who wrote the Happiness Hypothesis again?" and I'll say, "Jonathan Haidt" without a moment's hesitation. It feels like I've just won a prize. There's a hit of elation, a thrill of accomplishment. If playing Sudoku, and perhaps, as some say, bridge, can help keep the neurons and synapses firing, that's a palpable, rewarding bonus. Being challenged is pleasurable, and the results are gratifying as well. Good combo!

As I explore the subject, the question of cost-benefit arises. Clearly there are some things where the cost or price of not losing them is very high. Maybe too high to make the effort worthwhile. Take speaking German fluently.

I learned my German while falling in love, and became a fluent German speaker after I married my Austrian mountain climber love and moved to Europe, living in Germany and Austria.

Even now, twenty years later, I recall a lot of the language and structure. As soon as I start speaking, the words arise, as if out of nowhere, the sentence forms, and the thought makes it across. Sometimes, though, I have to simplify the sentence a bit, or the structure sounds clunky, or I find myself reformulating it in order to make it fit into the words I have accessible. I might be losing my ability to speak German fluently. But in order not to 'lose it', what would I have to do? Take a course, read in German, call up and talk to my friends or family in German on a regular basis. These are things I am not likely to do. And when I think about the consequences, I feel fine about my choice. I am confident that I will not lose the capacity altogether. And some falling off of my peripheral vocabulary is acceptable. For me, keeping it up, or expanding it, is not worth the trouble, time or energy.

Caring for my physical body, on the other hand, keeping as healthy, fit, flexible, and functional as I possibly can is a very high priority for me. My willingness to maintain my health is vigorous. Within limits, for sure. I'm willing to do a lot, but won't devote all my waking time and energy to it. And those limits may well vary as time goes on. But 'use it or lose it' is clearly part of my enthusiasm and motivation. And it feels good, inside and outside.

Another fitting 'use if or lose it' category is sexuality. I've heard warnings that, as time goes by, desire will wither and dry up, and that shriveling can occur in all manner of other areas as well. While some may find sex between older people disgusting to contemplate, and no doubt, the ads and models we are exposed to are young, buff and amply stacked or endowed, much has been written about the golden glow of sex in the golden years. Use it and you won't lose it. Losing the warmth and intimacy of sexuality certainly does seem a form of drying up. This doesn't sound appealing and I value exploring sensuous ways to experience intimacy as the years pass.

Spiritual growth is also, in my experience, very much about using or losing it. When we are living in our usual, patterned, lazily unconscious mode, we are not growing. When I act in habitual ways, unconsciously, automatically, I am simply running the same old programs, again and again. Making an ongoing effort to be aware, be in my body, be here, now, and conscious will enable me to open up and experience presence. But it takes commitment and practice.

'Use it or lose it' can evoke the image of a harsh disciplinarian, a critic—maybe even a well meaning one, and one purporting to be a friend. But this is the kind of friend we can all do without! Yet the phrase can also be an invitation to *'give it a go, see what happens.'* Reflecting on the two tones, and noticing where my priorities lie, is leading me to accept my own imperfections, and to stop pressuring myself. Who needs slave drivers! When I make choices more consciously, less hastily, and less out of fear, I find am taking more responsibility for my own life, and not striving to live up to cultural, or someone else's ideals or values. Take a walk in your garden, choosing whether to use it or lose it!

Related reading:
Brown, Byron (1998). *Soul Without Shame: A guide to liberating yourself from the judge within.* Boston: Shambhala
Chopra, Deepak (1993). *Ageless Body, Timeless Mind: The quantum alternative to growing old.* NY: Harmony Books
Crowley, Chris and Henry Lodge (2004). *Younger Next Year: A guide to living like 50 until you're 80 and beyond.* NY: Workman Publishing
Dreyer, Danny, Katherine Dreyer (2004). *Chi Running: A revolutionary approach to effortless, injury-free running.* NY: Simon & Schuster
Quackenbush, Thomas (1997). *Relearning to See.* Berkeley: North Atlantic Books

Reflections: *What primary affect does the 'use it or lose it' maxim have on you, fear or inspiration? In what areas of your life is 'use it or lose it' a sensible approach? What are some dimensions and facets of your life in which you are willing to invest time and energy to maintain? What are areas or skills you are willing to lose, or about which you are willing to become more loose?*

*"We are an endless moving stream in an
endless moving stream." Jisho Warner*

"Be infinitely flexible and constantly amazed." Jason Kravitz

Flow

Man, I like rollerblading. I didn't learn until quite late in life—in my sixties, to be exact. I thought it looked like splendid fun, but truth be told, it also seemed a bit scary. I had not skated much as a kid, on rollers or ice, and I have never much liked the feeling of too much speed, slipping and sliding, or not being able to stop on a dime. A friend of mine was given some rollerblades as a birthday gift by some co-workers. When Jason decided he wasn't going to take up the sport, but was going to return the blades for another, safer gift, I felt confirmed in my decision. Blading had a certain appeal, but I settled into 'no, it's not for me.'

When, a few months later Jason told me he had decided to keep his blades after all, and that he was quite enjoying them, I did a double take. If Jason could start at his age, I felt impelled to give it a try too. Not always recognizable as such, gifts come in many different forms!

I went to the nearest discount sports store, got quite a deal, and figured it was worth the financial outlay even if rollerblading didn't turn out to be my bag. While it was true that I found the prospect of gliding somewhat frightening, I also found it appealing. The bladers I had observed, even secretly envied, looked so smooth, so free. Transported in some way.

In my first efforts I was admittedly, intermittently, extremely awkward. I remember the first time I tackled the whole sea wall around Stanley Park in Vancouver, a good 10 km. On the smooth stretches it felt like gliding along a silk road. When it was rough, though, it was as though every tooth in my head was being individually rattled, I felt it up and down my entire spine. But even at that point, jolting between rough and smooth, jerking between silken and abrasive, there was a certain thrill to the experience: sensing and absorbing the sea, the forest, the beaches, the birds, the water falls, the ivy covered walls as they rolled by.

The first few months I fell down three times. I remember each one. Landed smack on my bottom, jarred my tail bone and injured my pride as well. I wondered about calling the whole thing off, but decided first to follow up on the store's offer of a couple of free lessons. There was enough valuable and intriguing in the experience that a couple of falls were not reason to abort entirely.

Clive was a great teacher. He modeled safety, wearing not only the protective wrist and knee gear, but a helmet as well. He was inclusive and didn't treat me like the slow learner I felt I was. I couldn't seem to really get the hang of the glide movement, wasn't able to balance on one blade, even with momentum, for ten seconds like others in the class could. I couldn't stop well (and actually injured my wrist by running into a wall when I didn't manage to stop in time), didn't have the intuitive feel for the arm swinging. My arms seemed to go the wrong way, and even when I watched those who looked smooth, I couldn't imitate it.

But after the lessons, I didn't fall down any more for a long time. Very slowly I began to gain comfort and confidence. I remember what seemed to be quite a steep hill on the east end of Ceperly Park. It was there I finally got the hang of the arm movements. I was leaning into the hill, working hard to climb, pushing up, leaning from side to side. At one point I noticed that my arms, just naturally, at last, without my knowing quite how, did the right thing. I could feel the shift. Ah, so this was the movement Clive had been trying to demonstrate, that I had seen others perform, but hadn't mastered myself. I was focused, alert. I hadn't 'done it,' it was just happening!

I still confine my blading to dry weather, mostly flat stretches, low traffic times, but I do move in and out of the barriers, on and off the curbs, up and down occasional hills and over some pretty rough patches with a certain ease and comfort. It is like sailing, flying; a cross between gliding and floating. It's action without effort. OK, not altogether without effort, but the little effort involved is in no relation to the outcomes and the benefits: the freedom, the smooth floating, the exhilaration of it.

What had begun as a personal challenge, and is exceedingly valuable as a form of low impact exercise, turns out to be an invitation to surrender to a broader and deeper flow. Which, long way around, is the point of this essay. Life is flow, which it always is, whether we are aware of it, in sync with it, or not. Including the bumps and batterings to which we are subjected.

But it can be illuminating to inquire into how we relate to the flow. Where is our awareness?

We can be very involved in any given activity—teaching, reading, balancing a checkbook, learning how to avoid falling down—and we can be quite focused and alert but not aware. How so? In a meditation retreat I once attended, the teacher used the example of a tight-rope acrobat. She might be excruciatingly absorbed, raptly fixed on her craft and task. But even focused and alert, she can be more or less running on automatic, doing well, even faultlessly, something in which she excels and is confident. In contrast, the deeper flow the teacher was describing has to do with our degree to which we actually bring full awareness to the activity, are embodied, fully present to what we're doing. Yes, focused and alert, yet also aware and richly in our bodies. There's a tingling of aliveness, as if I've added an extra dimension to my body and to my experience, at those times when I am in touch with myself, aware and present. It's like being inside myself as well as in the world.

Not to knock rapt absorption and excellence in a given activity! Yet we can delve even deeper when we partake of life with embodied awareness as well as focus and attention.

Fully engaging in rollerblading, in life, transforms me as well as the world I perceive, every time anew. When I am in touch with flow inside and let it work its alchemy, this transformation radically alters what I notice outside as well. In my usual, semi-automatic mode, the people I encounter are mere objects passing by. I might even find them obstacles of a sort. In the flow they can be fellow traveling souls, inviting a heart opening, a warm smile, the shared experience of a harbor seal peeking its nose out of the ocean, the crimson and purple striation of a fall sunset, the seagull grappling with the starfish, the squabbling of the crows and squirrels, the unexpected glimpse and grandeur of an eagle overhead. Ordinarily, people's faces are mundane and unnoteworthy. As flow, with awareness, they are portals: each one a different window into the moment, into their uniqueness, or possibly a mirror reflecting what's inside me.

Without knowing quite how it happens, not really being the doer, but nevertheless showing up, paying attention, being present, not being invested in any particular outcome, opening my mind and heart, giving up yet carrying on, I am rollerbladed, I am lived, I am in sync with the flow, I am flow.

Related Reading:

Castenada, Carlos (1969). *The Teachings of Don Juan: A Yaqui way of knowledge.* Berkeley: University of California Press

Kabat-Zinn, Jon ((1994). *Wherever You Go, There You Are: Mindfulness meditation in everyday life.* NY: Hyperion

Tolle, Eckhart (1999). *The Power of Now.* Vancouver, BC: Namaste Publishing

Weil, Simone (2001). *Waiting for God.* NY: HarperCollins

Reflections:

Consider a specific activity in your life, a familiar one that you sometimes do on automatic pilot. How do you experience this activity in a usual, everyday mode? Now describe what it is, or might be, like to be engaged in this activity when you are fully aware, present, in your body, in the flow? How might the insights affect your experience of the activity? Of your life?

*"Before I got married I had six theories about bringing
up children; now I have six children, and no theories."* John Wilmot

*"You are the bows from which your children as
living arrows are sent forth."* Kahlil Gibran

Push 'em Out of the Nest

There's a great blue heron rookery right outside my window. Every spring we see the parents gather, court, and build nests. We empathize with them as they lay and brood the eggs, protect them from the marauding raccoons and cruising eagles. It's a thrill when the young begin to hatch. Disheveled, they peer out over the edge of the nest.

The young herons continue to be very scruffy as they grow, through what would be the toddler stage, then adolescence. Then the days come that they start to fledge. The parents sit in the trees and watch while the young leave, one by one. One year there was a youngster who was still sitting on the edge of the nest long after all the others had flown. It seemed as though it just couldn't muster the courage. Nothing the parents had done, or could do, seemed to help. Each day we'd look out and see if it was still there. And the bird just sat there, day after day. It was heart wrenching and exciting at the same time. It illustrated the balancing act we parents and children have between holding on and letting go, between the capacity for closeness and the fostering of independence; nurturing and holding coupled with releasing and liberating.

At last, one day the heron was gone. Maybe it had flown off successfully, maybe an eagle got it, or it might have fallen to its death. I like to think it pulled together all of its resources, and gathering strength and courage from its parents' nurturing, it took off on its own. Maybe it will come back to the rookery next year to build a nest nearby.

I don't think we will ever be able to elucidate precisely the delicate balance between holding on and letting go that parents hope to strike as their children are becoming independent. It's as precarious and tippy as a fledgling heron on the edge of its nest. We can only do our best. And trust that it is good enough.

My parents believed in, and fully supported, their children's independence, yet they managed to create an environment where my friends and I were comfortable, and wanted to be. Maybe there's a link. If a home, and a parenting style, is nurturing, yet respectful of boundaries, it can create both a healthy independence *and* a desire to be there.

In spite of these felicitous moments in my early years, later in my life the balance didn't work so well.

Having their little ones leaving the nest was hard on my parents. Both children moved far away from home. I moved to Europe, my brother to California, and our parents were in Oklahoma. I only saw them once a year. Telephone calls were expensive and infrequent and saved for emergencies only. We wrote letters to stay in touch. When I compare this to the electronic video chats I am able to enjoy several times weekly with my son and his family who live in Austria, in addition to the phone calls which now cost only pennies, I realize how agonizing it must have been for my parents to be so far apart from their only grandchildren.

As much as my mother knew theoretically about the importance of 'letting go,' the practice of it was another matter. Interest in my life, suggestions and support that had been nurturing and warm when I was in grade school, turned into a drawn-out over-involvement in my life, well after I was 'out of the nest.' It was oppressive and damaging.

What might it take for parents to be able to 'let their children go,' to allow them to live *their* lives? One factor might be that the parents value their *own* lives. My mom was very talented and her life was full and comfortable, at least it appeared so from the outside. She was artistic, had friends and family, engaged in activities that contributed to others. Yet she was insecure and discontented, and was unable to let go of her children, perhaps in part because she did not value herself and her own life. She depended on, and was living through her children, an approach that led to a sense of loneliness and dissatisfaction in my mom, and pressure and difficulties for me.

Parenting is not perfect. There are bumps in the ride, and jostling along the way is the norm. But one quality that can help the letting go is tolerance of new and different ways of doing things. My daughter was barely six weeks old when we went to a seaside resort for some family time. A friend of my mom's was there, and when Joanne saw how I had Lisl perched beside me in a bouncy infant-seat, very close to where I was cooking on a hot stove, she said, "Gosh, parents today sure do things different from the way we did." There was no perceptible criticism in Joanne's remark. The tone was warm and she had a smile on her face. And that was the end of that.

I felt sort of smugly clever at how close my daughter was to the actions of everyday life, right there next to me while I was fixing dinner, compared to being stuffed away, as they typically were in my parents' generation, in a playpen, safe, certainly, but removed from the proximity that I valued. And I also took another look at whether my choice was smart. After all the seat was not very stable and the stove was very hot. I was left to make my own choices and take responsibility for my actions without feeling someone was looking over my shoulder.

This contrasts radically to an experience visiting my mom and dad when we lived in Europe. We were out for dinner and I was quite pleased that neither of my two kids was screaming loudly, demanding anything, or running around disruptively. When my mother observed their still rather rough version of table manners, she launched into a story of how she had recently seen a young girl drinking tea. She had used her napkin to wipe her lips in a dainty way, and had held her pinky finger up just the way Emily Post describes in her book of etiquette. Then my mother added, "Maybe your children can come to visit and learn to use their napkins properly." I could have chopped her head off. It was clear that she did not approve of the way I was doing things, and she thought she knew better. Not only did I experience no acknowledgment or acceptance, I did not even feel tolerated.

What else would help the process of parental letting go? Flexibility, perhaps? The ability to accept graciously, maybe even supportively, circumstances that have not turned out for, or with, your children the way you expected or wished. Counter example: When I phoned my parents to tell them about my carefully assembled plan for pursuing a graduate degree, my mom wailed, "Oh Jill, that's a shame. Can't you come back to the US for the program?" She burst into tears and hung up. I had hoped they would support the effort by coming over to help with the children while I was away as they had initially offered. Nope. Not when things turned out differently from their hopes and expectations.

A sense of humor—a helpful quality in many situations, not just in letting go. Yes, my family laughed and played together at home, but there was little lightness around the choices I made as a young adult: to marry someone not from my country, religion, or educational background, and ultimately to live abroad. All of these choices were received with hurt and criticism, not tolerance, flexibility or lightness. It was as though *my* choices were detrimental to *their* life.

Another consideration in walking the tightrope between encouraging independence on the one hand, and caring and protecting on the other, might be cultivating balance and proportion in core relationships. My mom was wise and nurturing in many ways. One day she told me, "Jill, don't put your children before your husband." It made a big impression even at the time, because

I sensed the personal struggle behind it. Like Cybil's advice, it was heartfelt, impassioned. "It's tempting to do," she said, "Children look up to us, we are important in their lives, and they do need our guidance. But don't attend to your children at the expense of your partnership." She didn't elaborate, and I was too young, self focused, and not in a relationship, to hear the urgency and recognize the wisdom of her words.

Through what my parents said and did, sometimes by the words and sometimes by example, or counter-example, I experienced that intricate web of emotions and reactions involved in the process of letting go. While it was detrimental to my independence and also to our relationship that my mother held on so tightly, and lived so much of her life vicariously through me, I empathize with her and the challenges parents face when the time comes to 'push 'em out of the nest.'

After all, who can manage always to be flexible, tolerant, light and balanced in daily life, especially when we feel that we are about to lose something very precious? No easy task.

Related reading:
Drew, Naomi (2000). *Peaceful Parents, Peaceful Kids: Practical ways to create a calm and happy home.* NY: Kensington Books
Faber, Adele and Elaine Mazlish (1990). *Liberated Parents, Liberated Children: Your guide to a happier family.* NY: Avon Books
Milne, A, A, (1994). *The Complete Tales of Winnie-the-Pooh.* NY: Dutton Children's Books
Satir, Virginia (1988). *The New Peoplemaking.* Mountain View, CA: Science and Behavior Books

Reflections: *What was your experience of the various ways in which you have let go of your little ones, if you had any? How did your parents 'let go' of you—or not? If someone were to ask your advice on how to relate to young people who are in the process of leaving home, and your advice on how to create a healthy, thriving relationship with adult children, what would you tell them?*

*"One doesn't discover new lands without consenting to
lose sight of the shore for a very long time." Andre Gide*

*"It kills you to see them grow up. But I guess it would kill you
quicker if they didn't." Barbara Kingsolver*

∾ల∾

Hold On or Let Go?

Having experienced much talk about 'pushing the chicks out of the nest' when I was growing up, I experienced a certain amount of internal resistance later on when I came across the advice to 'hold on to your kids.' Doesn't Kahlil Gibran's popular wisdom indicate that our children are not ours, that we must let them fly through us like an arrow through the bow?

Letting them go, even encouraging them to go, always seemed like the sensible approach. Plus they're going to leave anyway, and there's no stopping it. This focus on 'letting go' meant that, as a parent, I gave little attention, whether in disciplinary matters or in giving parental guidance, to 'holding on.' Nor did I pay much heed to the effect of my discipline and interactions on my children or on our relationship. To put it simply, I saw my job as a parent to encourage good and reasonable behavior and to prevent or punish bad. So 'hold on' as a philosophy of child raising and parenting was radical when I heard it, not very long ago, for the first time.

After much reflection, on my own childhood, my parenting, and having the gift of being close to my children's parenting, it now seems to me that it is possible both to hold on *and* to let go. So how can parents keep their children close to them, particularly during those difficult times when it would be so easy to push them away?

Most parents wonder, especially when we are at wit's end with our children's challenging behavior, what to do. How to deal with problematic behavior, the effects of peer pressure, outright defiance or rebellion? There used to be some fairly standard strategies that many parents used comfortably: spank them and send them to bed without supper, or at least send them off to their rooms. Or wash their mouths out with soap. Or ground them and dock their allowance. Not to say these largely punitive strategies 'worked,' but they were at least possibilities that many families considered. But with the development of new approaches, including the recognition of the importance of attachment, spanking and banishing in particular have come to be frowned on in many circles.

The shifts I observe in the next generation, as my children have become parents, are intriguing and in many cases heartening. One of the shifts can be summarized with the phrase 'hold on to your kids.' In dealing with difficult behaviors the newer goals can be seen as the effort to not just stop or prevent the offensive behavior, but to maintain or build a healthy and contactful relationship as well.

As a parent those challenging moments can be heart and gut wrenching. Sometimes we can feel like bashing those little monsters against a wall, if not cutting them in little pieces and flinging the pieces to the far winds. (Yes, I've felt all this and more!) When our children push our buttons, ignoring, for example, our efforts to be reasonable and fair, flying in the face of our requests to help around the house or be considerate of a sibling, it's awfully easy to want to push back and shove them away. Or bang their heads together and lock them in a dungeon. I know first hand, and have talked to other mothers who have felt the same way.

So how can we deal with problematic behavior and still maintain a loving relationship? It sounds great in principle, but it's not easy to implement in practice. It almost seems counterintuitive. Who wants to try to build a warm relationship with a kid who is shouting, as one of my grandkids did, "I hate you. You're mean and I wish you'd go away."

So what might 'hold on to your kids' mean in a case like the one above? It's easier to start with what it doesn't mean. Even when the behavior is challenging, unacceptable, 'hold on' means make every effort not to push your kids away. Don't discipline or guide them in ways that drive them away, or lead them to jump ship or close doors. Tall order indeed when as a parent, or even a grandparent, you are feeling hurt, angry, mistreated, and clueless on top of it all.

Sitting on the terrace with a young mother recently, whose son was four at the time, and desperately, if unconsciously, trying to establish his independence without jeopardizing the love he also needs, she was describing how her son, wouldn't talk, how he would pout, or run away, even hit and shout. How he'd often do exactly what his parents had asked please him not to do, as though out of utter spite. She said how excruciatingly frustrated and helpless she was feeling.

She'd tried sending him away, giving time outs, to make it clear the behaviors were not acceptable. And then she said that seemed to be making it worse for everyone. She realized that the distancing, in these exceedingly trying times, was creating an even bigger gap than was already there. Somehow she wanted to draw him closer, not send him away. So 'hold on,' yes, but how?

One example she came up with, instead of forcing him to take time alone in his room, would be to take her son in her arms, actively preventing him from the problematic behavior, and say, "Casey, I have to stop you from doing this until you can stop yourself."

There are no easy answers or pat solutions. Each parent has to find ways and means that seem an appropriate blend of taking action, keeping in mind the intention of connecting rather than distancing. This idea, hold on to your kids, is almost more an attitude than a set of rules, a philosophy affecting the way we think about our kids and ourselves when times are rough. Even if we don't know exactly what to do or how, we know we want to continue to maintain contact with our kids, not with harshness or out of bitter helplessness, but with love and connection.

My family was one where my friends liked to come over and have tea, hang out, chat with my parents. (Sometimes I got the feeling they liked my parents better than they liked me!) It was a homey place, comfortable, safe. When my friends were around there was a sense that my parents respected and liked them. My parents both treated young people as people, enjoyed their company, were willing to listen. It was an interesting paradox that my parents believed in letting their children be independent and fly the coop, yet they managed to create an environment where my friends and I enjoyed hanging out, at home and even with them.

It was good modeling for me, and I still appreciate their warmth and remember the gatherings with fondness. Still, when I had my own children I was not able to do the same. My kids went to other kids' homes. Even though we invited them, offered the basement for their parties, it was rare that they chose to be home. I believed that I was responsible for managing and molding their behavior (manners, chores, dealing with anger, peer pressure, drugs, homework). Yet I didn't have the paradigm of 'holding on,' building relationship at the same time.

One of the challenges with my children was my son's anger, which surfaced very early, when he was not more than four years old. His anger was a formidable force. It was all he could do not to throw or smash things. I sent him to his room. Pushed him away. Luckily though, I intuitively sensed the importance of not losing touch altogether, and we made the arrangement that when he was able, he'd come back and we'd talk about what had happened. In our case this worked well.

We experienced an emotional and relational roller coaster with our daughter, especially during the teenage years. Not that this is uncommon. We tried talking things out. Made deals and schedules around homework and chores. Nothing seemed to work. There was bitterness, tears, broken deals, frustration, trouble in school, and a damaged relationship between us. We changed schools, struggled with peer pressure and choice of friends.

I am gratified to report that we came through it all. A significant part of the shift is because at some point I recognized the importance of really listening, and finally learned and began to practice it! Yet, as I think back to these times, I wonder how it might have worked, through the challenging phases where children want and need to be independent, and themselves are pushing away, if I had known about, and added into my parenting tool kit, the relationship skills that 'holding on to your kids' implies.

Related reading:
Bailey, Becky (2000). *Easy to Love, Difficult to Discipline: The 7 basic skills for turning conflict into cooperation.* NY: HarperCollins
Faber, Adele and Elaine Mazlish (1999). *How to Talk So Kids Will Listen & Listen So Kids Will Talk.* NY: Collins
Nelson, Jane (1981). *Positive Discipline.* Fair Oaks, CA: Sunrise Press
Neufeld, Gordon and Gabor Mate (2004). *Hold On to Your Kids: Why parents need to matter more than peers.* Toronto: Knopf Canada

Reflections: *How did your parents' style of dealing with family difficulties affect the relationship between you and them, first as a child, then later as an adult? Was it a supportive, warm connection, or were you glad to escape? Or both? How did this relationship change over the years? If you could have an open conversation today, what would you like to say to your parents? If you are a parent yourself, how do you feel about your parenting style, and what would you do differently if you had it to do over again? Is there anything you would like to tell your children? If so, when will you do it?*

*"Even if our efforts of attention seem for years to be producing
no result, one day a light that is in exact proportion to
them will flood the soul."* Simone Weil

*"The first man to see an illusion by which men have flourished
for decades surely stands in a lonely place."* Gary Zukav

Really Letting Go: Surrender

What do you do when life starts to turn sour, seems to be derailing or getting crunchy? When things start to 'go south' for me, the first thing I have always done, until very recently, has been to make a plan. I made Plan A first, and for good measure, I would also develop a Plan B. For decades I didn't even realize I was doing this.

What do you do first thing when you wake up in the morning? For years, even on good days, I used to think forward, locate something positive—a tennis game, tea with a friend, some open space to read or exercise—and then I would feel myself coming together around the bright spot and would manage to get up and start the day.

And then there were those darker mornings when I'd wake up with a vague anxiety, a diffuse malaise, a greyness of spirit that was hard to define. I tried to deal with the churning inside by creating a plan. I'd go here, do that, call this person and take that trip. There. That felt better. Now there was some certainty again. I could face the future.

What is your strategy for getting through difficult times? My plan-making is a modus operandi for survival that I learned very early on. I had the early experience that I probably wasn't going to get what I really wanted so I made a decision, way back then, to try to figure out how to make things good and then set about making that happen. Or so I believed.

There are many ways that we as humans have developed to cope with our less than perfect worlds, and we develop these based on our early environments. While *my* primary coping mechanism is to plan, other people might take charge, try to be the boss or attempt to make things perfect; try their very hardest to please those around them. Some of us zone out and back off, or feel hurt and hard done by and try to get sympathy and be special. Or learn to excel, be the best. 'There, that'll show 'em!' we say. And these are just a few... there are many more.

Investigating these structures and patterns that are deeply grooved in our psyches, seeing how we often, largely unconsciously, resort to them over and over, is at first like going down a deep well. It can feel narrow and confining. Hopeless. 'Maybe I'll get swallowed up and won't be able to escape or find my way back home.' But if we stay with the exploration, we find that we learn more, we can begin to see that there is a thread we can unwind, that understanding our patterns can be extremely illuminating and freeing.

As I tell you about one of my habitual strategies, how it unwound, and where it led me, I invite you to feel into one of yours.

As far back as I can remember, I believed I couldn't trust that life could be counted on to give me what I thought I needed. It felt uncertain, open-ended; I had a swamp-like feeling of not knowing what was to come, that things would turn out all right. The next step I took I might fall in over my head, or start to sink, slowly but inexorably out of sight. The discomfort with confusion and not knowing led to a fundamental urgency to create some certainty, to try to have things turn out the way I pictured them. 'You just can't leave it to fate, I'd think. I better jump in here and figure it out. That'll be best. For us all.'

So it has happened that my partners, children and extended family, not to mention colleagues and friends, have experienced with some annoyance my attempts to 'make it happen' a certain way. I honestly believed that my intentions were good. It seemed fine to me, but it didn't change the irritation for those on the receiving end of my actions. When I learned that people felt very uncomfortable and experienced me as manipulative, I was surprised and hurt. 'Oh, no. Really? I just wanted people to get to know each other and have fun.' Or 'It was a perfect opportunity to take advantage of the great weather. How would anyone want to pass it up?' Or 'It's a beautiful sunset, and the canoe's already in the water. How could you not want to go out and enjoy it? Surely you'll change your mind.' How could these suggestions be manipulative?

So convinced was I that I had everyone's best interests in mind, and so familiar was the plan making to me, that it took me quite a while to be able to see with some objectivity what it must have been like to be involuntarily included in my plans. As I gradually penetrated more deeply into understanding my habits and patterns, and came to see that they were not only affecting me, but others as well, at first I thought 'Well that's *their* problem. I want the best for them. They'll see that sooner or later.' So when the letting go process started to roll, I had not only my own experience to release, but trying to control others' as well. But I'm getting ahead of myself here.

Most often we resort to our conscious or unconscious coping strategies when things turn difficult, although the 'fix' can become so prevalent that we do it in good times as well. But the easiest place to recognize it is to investigate what we do when time are tough.

As we follow the thread we can now ask, what is the effect of these strategies—whether planning, care-giving, fixing, bossing, spacing out, trying to be special, excelling? One result is that we invariably step out of the present moment. When my fear of uncertainly catapults me into the future, I am no longer paying attention to what is happening right now. Our strategies keep us from having to feel the distressing feelings, the discomfort of what is.

As I learned more about my particular experience, I saw that at core I did not accept, let alone trust the universe as it was unfolding. Since it was very challenging for me to trust that things will work out, I was holding on tight to a belief that I had to mess with my own experience, and the world out there, try to fix, think or plan my way to safety and well-being.

So what's to be done? Actually we ourselves can't *do* anything to make it different. As much as our egos struggle and effort, they are not able to master or manage the universe and its unfolding.

My evolving has been in letting go of planning and doing, giving up the belief and burden that I have to do it, that I need to manage the flow, for myself, for those in my life, and what is more, for the universe! Surrendering to the unfolding doesn't mean I am inactive. Far from it. But my actions now are not so much trying to cover over my fears, and to make things turn out as I see best, but to be aligned with what seems needed, with a larger flow, a sense of something grander, deeper, kinder, wiser than I could ever be.

When I wake in the morning now, my mind may race forward, and on some days my heart may be anxious. I notice the inclination to dart forward, to grasp for certainty, to manage. And, on good days, I take a breath and come back to the present, feel my body, notice my experience. It's actually simple. Not easy, but simple. If I am with myself, in the present moment, the first thing is to feel the feelings. Not avoid, fix, duck or run. Just notice.

What happens then we don't know, for we are part of an unfolding, an arising. I have experienced though, at times anyway, a growing ease with unknowing, with letting go of control. There can arise a sense of possibility, and trust that I am part of something larger and don't need to do it all myself. Sometimes there is even peace and openness, even excitement about the magic and potential of the present moment. Others, wiser than I, have documented how, when we let go, things tend to align in unexpected ways. May this be true for you.

Related reading:
Kornfield, Jack (1993). *A Path with Heart: A guide through the perils and promises of spiritual life.* NY: Bantam Books
Maitri, Sandra (2006). *The Spiritual Dimension of the Enneagram: Nine faces of the soul.* NY: Penguin
Ram Dass (2000). *Still Here.* NY: Riverhead Books
Sogyal Rinpoche (1993). *The Tibetan Book of Living and Dying.* NY: HarperCollins
Woollam, Ray (1985). *On Choosing with a Quiet Mind.* Duncan, BC: Unica Publishing Company

Reflections: *What are some specific coping strategies to which you resort in crunchy situations? Which of these habits or patterns are closest to your heart and your sense of yourself? Next time you find yourself in this pattern, take a breath and pay attention to what's going on inside. See if you can explore what would happen if you let go, of the pattern, of the outcome, of the belief that you're in control?*

"Like the moon, come out from behind the clouds! Shine."
The Buddha

*"Until you become yourself, what benefit can
you be to others? Harold Bloom*

Afterword

I f, dear reader, you have progressed to this page, you deserve
heartfelt thanks and warm appreciation for your time and
interest. I affectionately consider us fellow travelers, and
would be pleased if our paths cross on the journey to come.

The preceding essays have had a distinctly personal focus,
but they flow also out of the cultural, political, economic,
educational, and religious currents prevailing at the time. As we
conclude our trip together it seems fitting to mention some of
these larger factors. I think of Twiggy (need I say more?); the
Cold War and bomb shelters; fixed expectations about how to
look and what to aspire to. There was an aura of potential mutual
destruction between world powers, yet on a local scale, there
was a sense that in many ways, the situation was improving, we
should be able to make more of our lives than had our parents.

Yet women were second-class citizens in many areas.
Shadows and ambiguities. I am grateful for my father, my math
teachers, and the stimulating and supportive environment at the
women's college I attended, for moderating what could have
been severely limiting tendencies in my life. Yes, the Women's
Liberation Movement was growing. But I was already 21, and
many patterns and priorities were already established in my
life when, in 1963, Betty Friedan's Feminine Mystique was
published. My move to Europe (shortly after my first marriage

in 1965), where the women's movement was slower to take hold and more diffuse, served to distance me somewhat from pressing feminist as well as anti-war issues, and from the middle class, mid-western values, predominant when I was young.

But even overseas, freed perhaps a bit from familiar clinches, I did not find it easy to find my way. Cultural differences magnified this situation. My academic degree was not recognized in Europe, which added challenges and limited opportunities. Having had the benefit of an excellent education, I experienced pressure to find some measure of meaningful work; to contribute; to live up to my 'potential' and 'social expectations.' This caused inner and outer turmoil. Not in the same ways attempting to marry career and home life would challenge young women coming after, but turmoil nevertheless. I am also aware that the privileges I enjoyed—educational, cultural, financial, to name a few—in addition to contributing pressures of their own, also mitigated the effects of the some of the constraints I experienced, and created options. I am grateful for these gifts.

These, then, are some of the overarching issues and influences that shaped my perspectives and choices.

My hope is that your stories are now coming alive for you: that you have been challenged and encouraged to look at the kaleidoscope of your life through fresh eyes, seeing new patterns, colors, and textures, as well as perceiving familiar patterns and matters in different ways; that you might be discovering unfamiliar seeds or plants in your life garden, or that familiar seeds are now beginning to bear attractive and abundant fruit. Perhaps there are moments when the pieces that comprise the kaleidoscope are not separate and distinct, but join together in an ever changing, emergent flow—fresh, exquisite, intriguing, mysterious.

Related reading:

Adyashanti (2000). *The Impact of Awakening.* Los Gatos, CA: Open Gate Publishing

Albom, Mitch (1997). *Tuesdays with Morrie: An old man, a young man, and life's greatest lesson.* NY: Broadway Books

Almaas, A. H. *Two Heaps* (unpublished manuscript)

_____, *(*1986). *Essence: The Diamond Approach to inner realization.* York Beach, ME: Samuel Weiser, Inc.

_____, (1986) *The Void: Inner spaciousness and ego structure.* Berkeley: Diamond Books

_____. (1988). *The Pearl Beyond Price: Integration of personality into Being: An object relations approach.* Berkeley: Diamond Books

_____, (1998). *Facets of Unity: The enneagram of holy ideas.* Berkeley: Diamond Books

_____, (2002). *Spacecruiser Inquiry: True guidance for the inner journey.* Boston: Shambhala

_____, (2008). *The Unfolding Now: Realizing your true nature through the practice of presence.* Boston: Shambhala

Bachelard, Gaston (1994). *The Poetics of Space: The classic look at how we experience intimate places.* Boston: Beacon Press

Bailey, Becky (2000). *Easy to Love, Difficult to Discipline: The 7 basic skills for turning conflict into cooperation.* NY: HarperCollins

Baldwin, Christina (1991). *Life's Companion: Journal writing as a spiritual quest.* NY: Bantam Books

Barks, Coleman (1995). *The Essential Rumi.* NY: HarperCollins

Belenky, Mary, et al (1986). *Women's Ways of Knowing: The development of self, voice, and mind.* NY: Basic Books

Berry, Thomas. (1999). *The Great Work: Our way into the future.* NY: Random House

Blackmore, Susan (1999). *The Meme Machine.* Oxford: Oxford University Press

Bombeck, Irma (2005). *When God Created Mothers.* Kansas City: Andrews McMeel Publishing

Bolen, Jean (2001). *Goddesses in Older Women: Archetypes in women over fifty.* NY HarperCollins

Boorstein, Sylvia (1996). *Don't Just Do Something, Sit There.* San Francisco: Harper Collins

Brahm, Ajain (2005). *Who Ordered This Truckload of Dung? Inspiring stories for welcoming life's difficulties.* Boston: Wisdom Publications

Brown, Byron (1998). *Soul Without Shame: A guide to liberating yourself from the judge within.* Boston: Shambhala

Campbell, Joseph (1968). *The Hero with a Thousand Faces.* Princeton: Princeton University Press

Cameron, Julia (1982). *The Artist's Way: A spiritual path to higher creativity.* NY: Penguin Putnam

Castenada, Carlos (1969). *The Teachings of Don Juan: A Yaqui way of knowledge.* Berkeley: University of California Press

Chodron, Pema (1997). *When Things Fall Apart: Heart advice for difficult times.* Boston: Shambhala

Chodron, Thubten (2001). *Working with Anger.* Ithaca: Snow Lion Press

_____, (1999). *Taming the Monkey Mind.* Torrence, CA: Helan

Chopra, Deepak (1993). *Ageless Body, Timeless Mind: The quantum alternative to growing old.* NY: Harmony Books

Crowley, Chris and Henry Lodge (2004). *Younger Next Year: A guide to living like 50 until you're 80 and beyond.* NY: Workman Publishing

Dalai Lama et al (1992). *Worlds in Harmony: Dialogues on compassionate action.* Berkeley: Parallax Press

_____, Jeffrey Hopkins, trans. (2005). *How to Expand Love: Widening the circle of loving relationships.* NY: Simon & Schuster

Davis, John (1999). *The Diamond Approach: An introduction to the teachings of A. H. Almaas.* Boston: Shambhala

De Bono, Edward (1970). *Lateral Thinking.* NY: Penguin Books

De Botton, Alain (2002). *The Art of Travel.* NY: Vintage Books, Random House

Dillard, Annie (1987). *An American Childhood*. NY: Harper & Row

——, (1989). *The Writing Life*. NY: Harper & Row

——. (1999). *For the Time Being*. NY: Penguin Putnam

Dresser, Maureen (2005). *Multicultural Manners: Essential rules of etiquette for the 21st century*. Hoboken, NJ: John Wiley & Sons

Drew, Naomi (2000). *Peaceful Parents, Peaceful Kids: Practical ways to create a calm and happy home*. NY: Kensington Books

Dreyer, Danny, Katherine Dreyer (2004). *Chi Running: A revolutionary approach to effortless, injury-free running*. NY: Simon & Schuster

Eber, Dorothy ((1991). *Genius at Work: Images of Alexander Graham Bell*. Halifax, NS: Nimbus Publishing

Edwards, Betty ((1989). *Drawing on the Right Side of the Brain: A course in enhancing creativity and artistic confidence*. NY: G. P. Putnam's Sons

Eisler, Riane (1995). *The Chalice and the Blade: Our history, our future*. NY: HarperCollins

——, and David Loye (1998). *The Partnership Way: New tools for living and learning*. NY: HarperCollins

Elkins, James (2000). *How to Use Your Eyes*. NY: Routledge

Epstein, Mark (1995). *Thoughts Without a Thinker*. NY: HarperCollins

——, (1998). *Going to Pieces without Falling Apart: A Buddhist perspective on wholeness*. NY: Broadway Books

Faber, Adele and Elaine Mazlish (1990). *Liberated Parents, Liberated Children: Your guide to a happier family*. NY: Avon Books

——. (1999). *How to Talk So Kids Will Listen & Listen So Kids Will Talk*. NY: Collins

Forni, P. M. (2002). *Choosing Civility: The twenty five rules of considerate conduct*. NY: St. Martin's Press

Frankl, Victor (1984). *Man's Search for Meaning*. Boston: Beacon Press

Fromm, Erich (1956). *The Art of Loving*. NY: Harper & Row

Fulghum, Robert (2003). *All I Really Need to Know I Learned in Kindergarten*. NY: Random House

Giesel, Theodor (1971). *The Lorax*. NY: Random House

Gilbert, Elizabeth (2007).). *Eat, Pray, Love: One woman's search for everything across Italy, India and Indonesia*. NY: Penguin Books

Gilligen, Carol (1993). *In a Different Voice: Psychological theory and women's development*. Cambridge: Harvard University Press

Goleman, Daniel (1995). *Emotional Intelligence*. NY: Bantam Books

Gottman, John (1994). *Why Marriages Succeed and Fail: And how you can make yours last*. NY: Simon & Schuster

Gray, John ((1992). *Men Are from Mars, Women Are from Venus*. NY: HarperCollins

Haidt, Jonathan (2006). *The Happiness Hypothesis: Finding modern truth in ancient wisdom*. NY: Basic Books

Hardin, Garrett (1968). *The Tragedy of the Commons*. Science: 162(1968):1243–1248

Harper, Gary (2004). *The Joy of Conflict Resolution: Transforming victims, villains and heroes in the workplace and at home*. Gabriola Island, BC: New Society Publishers

Harris, Thomas (1969). *I'm OK, You're OK*. NY: HarperCollins

Hopkins, Jeffrey (2001). *Cultivating Compassion*. NY: Broadway Books

Huxley, Aldous (2004). *The Perennial Philosophy: An interpretation of the great mystics, east and west*. NY: Perennial Classics, HarperCollins

James, Ted and Wyatt Woodsmall (1988). *Time Line Therapy and the Basis of Personality*. Cupertino, CA: Meta Publications

Jampolsky, Gerald (1990). *Love is Letting Go of Fear*. Berkeley, CA: Celestial Arts Publishing

Jeffers, Susan (1987). *Feel the Fear and Do It Anyway*. NY: Ballantine Books

Kabat-Zinn, Jon ((1994). *Wherever You Go, There You Are: Mindfulness meditation in everyday life*. NY: Hyperion

Kater, Kathy (2004). *Real Kids Come in All Sizes: Ten essential lessons to build your child's self-esteem*.

NY: Broadway Books

Kinder, George (2000). *The Seven Stages of Money Maturity: Understanding the spirit and value of money in your life.* NY: Bantam Books

King, Stephen (2000). *On Writing: A memoir of the craft.* NY: Simon & Schuster

Kingsolver, Barbara (2007). *Animal Vegetable, Miracle: A year of food life.* NY: HarperCollins

_____. (1998). *The Poisonwood Bible.* NY: HarperCollins

Kornfield, Jack (1993). *A Path with Heart: A guide through the perils and promises of spiritual life.* NY: Bantam Books

_____, (1994). *Buddha's Little Instruction Book.* NY: Bantam Books

Korten, David (2006). *The Great Turning: From empire to earth community.* Bloomfield. CT: Kumarian Press

Krishnamurti, J. (1969). *Freedom from the Known.* NY: HarperCollins

Lau-Tsu (Stephen Addis and Stanley Lombardo, trans.) (2007). *Tau Te Ching.* Boston: Shambhala

Leopold, Aldo (1948). *The Sand County Almanac.* Oxford: Oxford University Press

Lerner, Harriet (1989). *The Dance of Anger: A woman's guide to changing the patterns of intimate relationships.* NY: Harper & Row

_____, (1989). *The Dance of Intimacy: A woman's guide to courageous acts of change in key relationships.* NY: Harper & Row

Lewis, Thomas, Fari Amini and Richard Lannon (2000). *A General Theory of Love.* NY: Random House

Lingis, Alphonso (1998) *The Imperative.* Bloomington, Indiana: Indiana University Press

Linnae, Ann ((1999). *Deep Water Passage: A spiritual journey at midlife.* Boston: Simon & Schuster

Macy, Johanna (1991). *World As Lover, World As Self: Courage for global justice and ecological renewal.* Berkeley: Parallax Press

Maitri, Sandra (2006). *The Spiritual Dimension of the Enneagram: Nine faces of the soul.* NY: Penguin

Mahler, Margaret (1975). *The Psychological Birth of the Human Infant: Symbiosis and individuation.* NY: Basic Books

Mauer, Robert (2004). *One Small Step Can Change Your Life.* NY: Workman Publishing

McDonnell, Jane (1998). *Living to Tell the Tale: A guide to writing memoir.* NY: Penguin Books

Meyers, Linda (2007). *Becoming Whole: Writing your healing story.* Berkeley: Two Bridges Press

Miles, Rosalind (1988). *The Women's History of the World.* London: Paladin Grafton Books

Milne, A, A, (1994). *The Complete Tales of Winnie-the-Pooh.* NY: Dutton Children's Books

Mindell, Arnold (1995). *Sitting in the Fire: Large group transformation using conflict and diversity.* Portland, OR: Lao Tse Press

Moore, Thomas (1994). *SoulMates: The mysteries of love.* NY: Harper Perennial

Murdock, Maureen (1990). *The Heroine's Journey: Woman's quest for wholeness.* Boston: Shambhala

Needleman, Jacob (1994). *Money and the Meaning of Life.* NY: Doubleday

Nelson, Jane (1981). *Positive Discipline.* Fair Oaks, CA: Sunrise Press

Nemeth, Maria (1999), *The Energy of Money: A Spiritual Guide to Financial and Personal Fulfillment.* NY: Ballantine Books

Neufeld, Gordon and Gabor Mate (2004). *Hold On to Your Kids: Why parents need to matter more than peers.* Toronto: Knopf Canada

Nisargadatta, Sri Maharaj (1973). *I Am That.* Durham, NC: Acorn Press

Oliver, Mary (1986). *Dream Work.* NY: Atlantic Monthly Press

_____, (2004). *Long Life.* Cambridge, MA: Da Capo Press

Peck, M. Scott (1798). *The Road Less Traveled: A new psychology of love, traditional values and spiritual growth.* NY: Simon & Schuster

Psaris, Jett and Marlena Lyons (2000). *Undefended Love.* Oakland, CA: New Harbinger Publications

Pransky, George (2001). *The Relationship Handbook: A simple guide to more satisfying relationships.* LaConner, WA: Pransky and Associates

Quackenbush, Thomas (1997). *Relearning to See.* Berkeley: North Atlantic Books

Ram Dass (1978). *Be Here Now.* Kingsport, TN: Hanuman Foundation

_____, (2000). *Still Here.* NY: Riverhead Books

Redfield, James (1993). *The Celestine Prophecy*. NY: Warner Books

_____, (1996). *The Tenth Insight: Holding the vision*. NY: Warner Books

Remen, Rachel Naomi (2006). *Kitchen Table Wisdom: Stories that heal*. NY: Penguin Books

Richardson, Ronald (1995). *Family Ties That Bind: A self-help guide to change through family of origin therapy*. North Vancouver, BC: International Self-Counsel Press

Rosenberg, Marshall (1999). *Nonviolent Communication: A language of compassion*. Encinitas, CA: PuddleDancer Press

Ruiz, Don Miguel (1997). *The Four Agreements: A practical guide to personal freedom. A Toltec wisdom book*. San Rafael, CA: Amber-Allen Publishing

Sandburg, Carl ((1922). *Rootabaga Stories*. NY: Harcourt Brace & Co.

Sanguin, Bruce (2007). *Darwin, Divinity, and the Dance of the Cosmos*. Kelowna, BC: Wood Lake Publishing

Sarno, John (1998). *The Mindbody Prescription: Healing the body, healing the pain*. NY: Warner Books

Satir, Virginia (1988). *The New Peoplemaking*. Mountain View, CA: Science and Behavior Books

Schaef, Anne Wilson (1992). *Women's Reality: An emerging female system in a white male society*. NY: HarperCollins

Schaefer, Carol (2006). *Grandmothers Counsel the World: Women elders offer their vision for our planet*. Boston: Shambhala

Schucman, Helen and William Thetford (1985). *A Course in Miracles*. Tiburon, CA: Foundation for Inner Peace

Schwartz, Richard (1997). *Internal Family Systems Therapy*. NY: The Guilford Press

Schwartz, Tony (1995). *What Really Matters: Searching for wisdom in America*. NY: Bantam Books

Sheehy, Gail (1976). *Passages: Predictable crises of adult life*. NY: Bantam Books

Sheilds, Carol, Marjorie Anderson, eds. (2003). *Dropped Threads 2: More of what we aren't told*. Toronto, ON: Vintage Canada

Sinetar, Marsha (1986). *Ordinary People As Monks and Mystics: Lifestyles for self-discovery*. Mahwah, NJ: Paulist Press

Smith, Huston (1982). *Beyond the Post-modern Mind*. NY: Crossroad Publishing

Sogyal Rinpoche (1993). *The Tibetan Book of Living and Dying*. NY: HarperCollins

Swimme, Brian and Thomas Berry ((1992). *The Universe Story*. NY: HarperCollins

Tannen, Deborah (1990). *You Just Don't Understand: Women and men in conversation*. NY: Ballantine Books

_____, (1986). *That's Not What I Meant: How conversational style makes or breaks relationships*. NY: Ballantine Books

Taylor, Jill Bolte (2008). *My Stroke of Insight*. NY: Riverhead Books

Thich Nhat Hanh (1992). *Peace is Every Step: The path of mindfulness in everyday life*. NY: Bantam Books

_____, (1996). *Breathe! You Are Alive*. Berkeley: Parallax Press

_____, ((2005). *Being Peace*. Berkeley: Parallax Press

_____, (2001). *Anger: Wisdom for cooling the flames*. Berkeley, Parallax Press

Thomas, William (2007). *What are Old People For?: How elders will save the world*. Acton, MA: Vanderwyk & Burnham

Thoreau, Henry (2004). *Walden*. Princeton: Princeton University Press

Tolle, Eckhart (2005). *A New Earth: Awakening to your life's purpose*. NY: Penguin Group

_____, (1999). *The Power of Now*. Vancouver, BC: Namaste Publishing

_____, (2003). *Stillness Speaks*. Vancouver, BC: Namaste Publishing

Tulku, Tarthang (1977). *Time, Space, and Knowledge: A new vision of reality*. Emeryville, CA: Dharma Publishing

Twist, Lynn (2003). *The Soul of Money: Reclaiming the wealth of our inner resources*. NY: W.W. Norton

Weil, Simone (2001). *Waiting for God*. NY: HarperCollins

Welwood, John (1996). *Love and Awakening: Discovering the sacred path of intimate relationship*. NY: HarperCollins

_____, (2006). *Perfect Love, Imperfect Relationships: Healing the wound of the heart.* Boston: Shambhala

Wilber, Ken (2000). *A Theory of Everything: An integral vision for business, politics, science, and spirituality.* Boston: Shambhala

_____. (1996). *A Brief History of Everything.* Boston: Shambhala

_____. (1995, 2000). *Sex, Ecology, Spirituality: The spirit of evolution.* Boston: Shambhala

Wilder, Barbara (1999). *Money is Love: Reconnecting to the sacred origins of money.* Longmont, CA: Wild Ox Press

Williamson, Marianne (1993). *A Woman's Worth.* NY: Ballantine Books

Wolff, Robert and Thom Hartmann (2001). *Original Wisdom: Stories of an ancient way of knowing.* Rochester, Vermont: Inner Traditions

Woollam, Ray (1985). *On Choosing with a Quiet Mind.* Duncan, BC: Unica Publishing Company

Zinn, Howard (2002). *The Power of Nonviolence: Writings by advocates of peace.* Boston: Beacon Press

Readers' comments about BECOMING

"The candor and humor are truly engaging, the rhythm lively, and the stories make me want more!" - Margit H.

"BECOMING will be a valuable resource for many people on the journey and give reluctant travelers the courage to take their first steps. I love the frankness and openness and how clearly the author describes her journey through an issue to a new reality." - Carli S.

"It is well written, poignant, and has that down-to-earthiness feel to it. I also loved all the quotes that are used. They are exquisite." - Nitsa M.

"The author shares the gems of a self-reflective journey... Her insights and engaging style carry the reader toward lessons learned, perhaps not always easily... Jill takes us on a journey to the depths and helps us become aware of our own process of becoming." - Kathy B.

"I love the short chapters, each with a big message. I am reflecting lots. It feels familiar and personal and important." - Pru M.

"It is a delightful combination of reminiscence, inspiration and truth telling.... I found myself laughing in recognition when the author described her childhood and dealing with other people's expectations." - Sue A.

"The 'reflections' at chapter end launched us into a great conversation about who influenced us in childhood outside of our parents. Thank you again for writing such an experiential book." - Martine C.

"I've found so much that speaks to me... The section on different filters and how our life looks through them was very relevant to me right now....it's nice to have a reminder that you can look at it differently!" - Lisa R.